ONE BOY'S AMAZING STORY OF SURVIVAL

ON TWO FEET AND WINGS

ABBAS KAZEROONI

This book is based on real events that happened to me
a long time ago when I was a child. To write it for you
I have simplified some events and changed some details.
—Abbas Kazerooni

Published by Skyscape, New York

www.apub.com

Amazon, the Amazon logo, and Skyscape are trademarks of Amazon.com, Inc., or its affiliates.

ISBN-13: 9781477847831 (hardcover)
ISBN-10: 1477847839 (hardcover)
ISBN-13: 9781477820377 (paperback)
ISBN-10: 147782037X (paperback)

Cover design by Sammy Yuen
Book design by Ryan Michaels

Library of Congress Control Number: 2014933778

Printed in the United States of America

First published in 2008 as *The Little Man* by Tate Publishing, USA
Published in 2011 by Hachette India
Published in 2012 by Allen & Unwin, Australia

In loving memory of my mother,
Marzieh Kazerooni

TEHRAN

ONE

I t was a typical spring day in Tehran—hot, dusty, nothing special—when my life turned upside down. Reza, a driver shared by several families to take kids to school and back, had just dropped me off at home, and I was worrying about what I thought was a big problem: a rip in my trousers from a lunchtime soccer game.

The number of trousers my mother had mended was now beyond count. I knew I was in trouble, so I decided to consult my strongest ally: Mamanjoon, my grandmother.

She greeted me at our huge black wooden door by pinching my face, and to my disgust, planting two wet kisses on both cheeks with the usual, "I'm so happy you're home, my darling. Are you hungry?"

Normally, I would have said something like, "No thank you, Mamanjoon; I have to do my homework first." Even though my mother called me her mischievous little monkey, I was a closet geek. I always had to do my homework before I could relax or eat.

But on this particular day, I walked in with my head down, a sulky look in my big brown puppy-dog eyes. When Mamanjoon asked what was the matter, I pointed to the trousers.

"It's okay, my darling," she murmured. "I'll mend them for you. It will be our little secret."

Like a ferret, I scuttled to my room, trying to avoid both my mother and my father. As I crossed our large, mostly empty living room, my parents were so deep in conversation that they didn't notice me. For a second, I wondered what was going on, but then I hurried to my bedroom, happy that I had escaped notice.

I liked doing my homework in my bedroom. It always stayed cool because of its very high ceiling. It was a spacious room, much too big for me, with almost no furniture. My small bed stood in one corner, next to the radiator. In the winter, I would squeeze my toes in between the rails of the radiator to warm them. Above my bed was a huge window, nearly up to the ceiling. It looked out on our back garden, which led to an orchard divided into sections, each with a different type of tree: apple, cherry, pomegranate, and orange. I liked the orange trees best. They would fruit every year without fail, the oranges hanging like bright balls on heavy, dipping branches. On hot summer days, when the sun was too strong for me to play outside, I would jump onto my bed and gaze at those trees, their leaves shining golden in the sunlight.

In the opposite corner of the room was my favorite possession, a wooden desk with its matching stool. It had a top that flipped open, and I stored my books inside. But the best part was a secret drawer where I kept all my treasures: my favorite pen, my notepad with my scratchy calculations, and of course, my piggy bank, until I had hidden it outside. I knew just how much was in it to the exact *rial*.

I wasn't really into toys; I preferred playing with my plastic soccer ball and trying to make extra pocket money by any means possible. There were shops at the end of our street where I would go and pester the shopkeepers to let me run errands for money. At first they would resist, but I was persistent, so finally they would give in, asking me to sweep outside their shops or clean the windows—anything that would keep me quiet for half an hour.

If I had liked toys, I think I would have been disappointed. Ever since I could remember, Iran had been at war with Iraq. In wartime, everyone struggles to get by. But while my parents were not well off, our family had been rich once. This very house had been a grand mansion with lavish furnishings. I had heard stories and seen pictures of beautiful Persian carpets, priceless porcelain antiques, oil paintings of my family's ancestors that had covered entire walls, and gold-plated chandeliers that would light a room like a million stars . . . But these things were no longer ours.

My almost empty room had once been my grandfather's office, crowded with a desk and many stacks of paperwork. My father told me that my grandfather had loved looking out the window at the orchard, too. I grew up listening to stories about our family's past. Grandfather was one of the richest men in Iran. Our family was so famous that a television-show producer even made a twenty-four-part series about us!

My great-grandfather had started the Kazerooni "dynasty."' He was a self-made millionaire who, in his time, had a hold over nearly all the businesses in southern Iran, ranging from owning the butcher's shop just down the street to running the local shipping-dock unions. When the British invaded Persia at the turn of the twentieth century, the government did not fight them, but my great-grandfather funded guerrillas to put up an opposition!

By the time my father became head of the family, we were mingling with royalty and important government officials. Then the ayatollahs came into power and everything changed. Due to my father's connections with the previous regime— the Shah's rule—the ayatollahs confiscated most of my family's properties and assets. Many of the Shah's followers were executed; others were ostracized—no one spoke to them or conducted business with them. According to my father, we were lucky to be alive.

Despite the fact that we no longer enjoyed the luxuries we'd had earlier, the accounts that Baba gave me of those times were very important to me. This was what I bragged most about at school. If you know anything about Persians, then you will know that the art of boasting is drummed into us from a very early age. Not that I needed any encouragement. I had never experienced this glorious past, but that never stopped me from strutting and preening in its leftover shine.

So there I was in my room a bit later on that hot day, happy that I had avoided trouble over my trousers. My homework was done, but there was no chance of playing soccer against the wall, as my parents were close by in the living room, still talking in hushed tones. I sat for a while on my bed, looking out of the window, but soon I felt restless and decided to find out why Baba and Maman hadn't noticed me that afternoon.

At the door to the living room, I lay on my stomach as quietly as I could, peering around the corner. The large room was as sparsely furnished as mine. In the distant corner was an old white sofa where my parents sat, deep in conversation. A television on a stand was in front of the sofa. Above the television were three family portraits: my father, my grandfather, and my great-grandfather. The other walls were bare, except for the stains left behind by the frames of old paintings. A few baby pictures of me stood about on the odd shelf. There was nothing to block my view of my parents. That meant I had to be careful, as they could easily have seen me.

My father looked worried.

This was unusual. For a short man he had a strong presence. My mother was at least three inches taller than him, but he always seemed to be in charge. He would stroke his commanding mustache and brush his graying hair lightly as he listened to me, always calm yet authoritative. Maman lost her temper much more quickly and more often, and yet, she seemed vulnerable.

On that day, though, my father looked like a completely different man. I watched as he leaned toward my mother. "You know they won't give me a passport, don't you?"

The answer was obvious. Even I knew that my father's passport had been confiscated by the new regime. He had told me that the ayatollahs didn't want him to leave the country. He didn't explain why, but I read between the lines and figured that there was a political reason. I used to love it when he told me things like that. Afterward, he always made me promise not to mention any of it in public, as it was really dangerous for the whole family. It made me feel all grown-up—like a man—that my father trusted me with this vital information.

"Yes, I know," my mother replied as she brushed her shoulder-length auburn hair with her velvet-covered hairbrush.

"Well, you have to leave with Abbas, then."

My ears pricked up. What was he talking about? Where were we going? Passport? Were we going abroad?

At first, I was excited. This was what my friends and I would boast about most often: who would go abroad first. Only rich, important people traveled out of Iran, and I was delighted that I might beat my friends to it.

My mother's reaction certainly didn't match mine. I couldn't decide if she was sad or angry or both, but I knew she looked really upset, like she might cry. I hated seeing her like that.

"We have to get Abbas out of the country, my darling," Baba said again.

"He's nine, for God's sake," Maman answered, her voice full of emotion. "Just nine."

"That's exactly why we have to get him out now."

"How will he cope? He is too young to understand, Karim." She was beginning to cry.

Too young? I thought, indignant. *Just you try me.*

My father stopped to look at her. He wiped her tears away with his checked shirtsleeve and continued, "They've reduced the recruitment age to eight, Marzieh. You saw Meenoo yourself the other day. Her son was brought back in a coffin, and for what? How old was he—thirteen?"

"Twelve."

"Well, there you go. You're arguing my point for me."

I couldn't believe what he'd just said. Recruitment into the army was a hot topic of conversation, and I knew several children who had been signed up, including Pejman, the twelve-year-old son of Meenoo. My father always made him an example of what could happen to me. Pejman had been drafted. And now he was dead.

At school we were told we would go to paradise if we died in the war. My father always begged me not to listen, and so I didn't. He told me recruitment was a sad thing, and also stupid. If I'd repeated any of this in public I would have been caned until I bled, and my father would have been whipped for sure, if not thrown into prison and killed.

There was no hope that someone would be presumed innocent until proven guilty, or given a fair trial. My Uncle Kami had been on a motorcycle one day when there was an assassination attempt on one of the most important ayatollahs in Iran. One of the shooters was reported to be wearing a blue shirt and riding a motorbike. My uncle had the bad luck to be wearing a green shirt and be riding his motorbike in the vicinity. He was imprisoned for more than two years—tortured, his legs broken. I remember that when he was finally let out, he was still on crutches. We lived in a totalitarian state where the dictatorship would not tolerate even the slightest resistance or insubordination.

But recruiting eight-year-olds? I was already nine. I'd always known I might have to go to war but never thought it could be so soon. I froze with fright. I didn't want to leave my mother, and I certainly didn't want to die.

"Eight?" my mum said. "Are you sure?"

"Positive," he said sadly. "Bahman told me, and he gets it straight from the top." Bahman was one of my father's oldest friends. He had somehow worked himself in with the new regime and was partly responsible for our family being left alone.

In my nine years, my father had never revealed himself to be an emotional man. I had seen him lose his temper only once. That was on a hot summer's day several years ago. I had been on my bike, riding in the small, pothole-ridden streets. Eventually, I'd come to an old mulberry tree that my friends and I often climbed, which gave us an enviable view of Tehran. I was alone this day. I left my bike at the base and climbed to the top like a chimpanzee. I knew no fear. As I sat there, looking out across the city, I heard my father from below: "If you don't come down, someone will take this bike."

"It'll be fine, Baba. Just leave it."

"Really?" he muttered disapprovingly. "Well, God help you if you're wrong."

Thirty minutes later, I did come down. My bike wasn't there. My stomach dropped. This must be a sick joke. I hoped desperately that my father had taken it with him. I trembled all the way home.

My father was in the kitchen drinking tea when I arrived. He knew before I could speak. He read it on my face.

"You lost it, didn't you?"

I had no time to nod before he was out of his chair, screaming, "You spoiled little brat." He slapped me so hard it knocked me off my feet. "You're going to have to learn the value of money. I sweat every day so you can have all your luxuries, and this is how you show your gratitude?"

"But—"

"No buts. You're going to have to learn the hard way."

He slapped me to the floor again. I could see the pure unadulterated anger in his eyes. Everything was happening in slow motion. I felt so small and insignificant as all his manly strength overpowered me. Baba took off his belt and began whipping me with it. The memory of the buckle vibrating across my back has stayed with me to this day. Only when my mother forced him away and the imminent danger had passed did I begin to cry. Before that, I was in too much shock. I cried myself to sleep. Only when I woke did I really feel the pain of that beating. My father refused to speak to me for a month. That hurt me more.

Now was the first time I had seen my father sad. I guessed it was because he knew that if he sent me out of Iran, he would have to be separated from me.

My mother wanted to say something, but she bit her lip and stayed silent. My father edged closer toward her and stroked her cheek with the back of his right hand, as he so often did when he wanted to show her affection.

"They'll pick on people like us first, Marzieh. You know they will."

"But he's only nine, for God's sake," she said as she broke down sobbing.

Suddenly, Mamanjoon entered the room, quite oblivious to what was going on. She was ninety-five, but active for her age. She wobbled closer to the pair of them, using her walking stick. Her white hair fell across her glasses as she looked at my father and said, "Tea, anyone?"

"No, thanks, Maman," he said, looking flustered. "Maybe later."

He turned away and continued to stroke my mother's cheek while Mamanjoon stood there looking puzzled.

After a long silence, Mamanjoon spoke again: "Are you sure you won't have any tea? It's freshly brewed!"

My mother raised her teary eyes with studied politeness and spoke with her last ounce of patience. "No, thank you, Mamanjoon. Really, we're fine."

Mamanjoon sighed heavily, as if she'd been seriously offended, and exited, hobbling dramatically. Mamanjoon's entrance had been a distraction, but now my parents leaned toward each other again. I could see pain in their eyes as I watched, my face in my hands, as I lay sprawled out in the hallway. I hoped Maman would make everything all right. She always did.

Baba spoke very quietly into Maman's ear, but I could hear everything. The lack of furniture made their voices echo sharply, like an ominous wind. "You have to go ahead with Abbas, and I'll make my own way later." He paused for a reaction but continued when he didn't get one, ". . . somehow."

My mother's eyes flashed with tears. "We can't leave without you," she murmured.

I wanted to run across the room and comfort her. I had not known any other life, and the thought of change terrified me. Nevertheless, I could see that my father had made up his mind.

"You have to go, Marzieh. It's for Abbas's sake," he repeated. He meant what he said. I knew my father.

My mother made a last effort to change his mind as she wept, "But you are my husband and Abbas's father."

My stomach felt as if it were on fire. I was hurting because my mother was hurting. I am sure my father was in pain too, but at the time I couldn't tell. His tone was so matter of fact.

"Abbas has to come first. If that means we have to be separated for a while, then so be it," he said. "You have to take him, Marzieh. You have to take him."

And that was that.

My mother collapsed in his lap. My father held her and spoke gently into her ear. I remember him mouthing words I could not hear. I recall Mamanjoon, reappearing in the doorway, wiping away her tears, as she must have been listening, too.

I couldn't watch any longer. I went to my room and lay on my bed, and before I knew it, I had cried myself to sleep.

The next morning I woke up before my alarm rang. I was facing the wall next to my bed as I opened my eyes. I knew it was too early for school, but something compelled me to turn over. Across the room, I saw my father looking at me as he played with his worry beads, a sign that he was stressed. Usually, the tenser he was, the more he played with them. You could hear the beads clicking one by one in an endless cycle.

I squinted and rubbed my eyes. "Morning, Baba."

"Good morning," he muttered back, his voice full of emotion, his face sad. He had never looked at me like that before. Something wasn't right. I sat up and gave him a questioning look. He stayed silent and carried on playing with his beads. I glanced at the clock and then back at him again. "What's wrong, Baba? It's only five. I have another hour before school."

"I know," he replied. Then he was silent. He seemed to be searching for the right words.

I decided to make it easier for him. "Are we leaving soon, Baba?"

A little smile crept up the side of his mouth as he answered with a nod.

"When?"

"As soon as possible, Abbas," he said. "As soon as possible." I waited for him to continue. His next words took me by surprise. "You're not going to school today," he said. "You're staying home to help me and your mother."

"Why?"

"We have to prepare you for the trip. You may have to leave at any time."

My father's tone had changed—become brusque and businesslike. He was talking to me like an adult. He knew me very well; he knew that's what I liked.

"We'll tell the school you're unwell," he said. "We'll tell them you're really ill and cannot attend any classes."

"But my friends will see me," I said. My friends would usually come to our house and knock on the door, and I would go out and play soccer with them until dark. Sometimes we would ride our bikes or play hide-and-seek.

My father was quiet for a few moments. I guessed his next sentence would not please me.

"I'm sorry, Abbas, but you can't go out of the house again until the day we leave."

I stared at him, horrified. "What about my friends?"

"You can't see them again, Abbas. It's too dangerous." His voice was tinged with compassion, as he must have known the enormity of what he was asking me to do. All my joy came from playing with my friends.

"I'll say goodbye for you," he said. "If they find out we're taking you out of school for any reason other than illness, they'll know we're up to something."

I considered his words carefully before responding. "You're not coming with us, are you?" I knew it, but I wanted to confirm it.

"No," he said very simply. "I'm not."

"Is that because they took away your passport?" I asked quietly.

"Yes." Then he paused and reached up and touched my messy, uncombed hair. "I can't let them drag you into the army, Abbas. I won't let it happen."

"But I might not see you again," I said.

"If you go to war, you definitely won't see me again." He went on, "It's going to get tough in the next couple of weeks, Abbas."

"How do you mean?" I asked. "How much harder could this get?"

"Well, we have to sell a lot of things," he said. "Things precious to us."

"Why?"

"Because we have to buy your tickets and get money for you to use later," he replied.

I stopped asking questions then, so that I could come to terms with what Baba had told me. I looked out of my window, holding back my tears. I stared straight into the peachy-orange ball of the sun just rising above the pine trees at the back of the garden. It was a beautiful morning, but somehow everything looked ugly and threatening.

"Are you all right?" my father asked, tapping me on the shoulder.

I turned around and nodded. "Where are we going?" I asked.

"You and your mother will leave for Turkey, and there you will apply for a British visa. When you get it, you will go and stay with your cousin, Mehdi, who will help you until your mother gets on her feet, and then you will wait for me there." I took a deep breath as I tried to take all of this in.

"What are we going to have to sell, Baba?" I asked quietly.

I saw surprise in his eyes. I think he was impressed that I was thinking along those lines rather than about my friends. He laid a hand on my shoulder and stroked his short-cropped beard as he spoke. "I'll be honest with you, Abbas," he said. "Our lives will change dramatically in the next few weeks. All the little luxuries that we take for granted will have to go; for instance, the television will have to be sold."

"They only show religious stuff anyway," I said cheerfully. I could see that he appreciated my positive attitude.

"All of your mother's jewelry," he continued, "all of Mamanjoon's too, and the stove, the pots, the pans, and . . ."

"And what?" I asked.

"And your desk, too, perhaps," he said, waiting for a reaction. He didn't get one, though. I wasn't happy about it, but I didn't show it.

"Why are we going to Turkey?"

"That's the only place you can go where you can try for a visa to get into England. Money," he added, "will be very short from now on. We have to cut out treats, expensive food, or anything that isn't essential. Do you understand me?"

I nodded.

"You'll be looking after Maman for me in Turkey, Abbas. I won't be the head of the family anymore; you will."

I usually loved to hear that I was the head of the family and the man of the house, but this time around it didn't feel so good.

Baba patted my head. "You can do that for me, can't you, buddy?"

I nodded, because if I had spoken, I think I would have become hysterical. Eventually, I took a deep breath as my father had taught me to do if I was upset, and then I asked, "If I'm not allowed to leave the house, Baba, then what will I do during the day?"

"There are things that you and your mother will need to know about Turkey—about Istanbul, where you will stay. I will try to teach you as much as I can."

I looked at him and dared to ask, "And how do you know these things, Baba?"

I had never questioned my father like this before. But he merely replied, "I have friends everywhere."

That I couldn't argue with. People all over Iran knew of my father. I had traveled with him on several trips and, without exaggeration, could say that sometimes people nearly worshipped him. This was especially true in southern Iran, where he had employed thousands of people in the past.

"When we're not talking about life in Istanbul, you can help me pack things so that I can sell them." That brought a smile to my face, because once again he had asked for my help. Before now, I had only dreamt of the day when my father would ask for my assistance. He could see I was satisfied. "Come on, Abbas, go back to sleep. You can sleep in today."

"And tomorrow!" I replied cheekily.

"We'll see," he said with a smile as he tucked me in. Then he kissed me on the forehead and left the room.

I wasn't sure why Baba was telling me all this so early in the morning. I wondered if he had wanted to speak to me about the trip before my mother could. He would have known I would jump at the thought of being grown-up and handling responsibility.

I certainly took his bait.

Two

When I woke up later and strolled into the kitchen to get some breakfast, I saw my mother sitting alone at the small wooden table that was like an island in our large, mostly empty kitchen. I could see she had been crying, but she smiled when she saw me.

"Morning, darling. Would you like some breakfast?"

I nodded. She walked, as if on autopilot, to the small white fridge next to the doorway, took out the *lavash* and *panir*, and put them on the table. Then she went to the stove, poured me a glass of tea, and sat down next to me.

It was not unusual for her to watch me eat, but this time was different. She knew that my father had spoken to me, and she looked worried. At the same time, all I could think about was whether she was all right. I spread the panir on the thin white lavash while I thought about what to say.

"Are you okay, Maman?" I burst out, finally.

She reached out and held my hand as she spoke. "Yes, I'm fine, Abbas."

I took a bite and started chewing slowly as I watched her. She looked like she was trying to build up the courage to talk about what was going to happen.

"Are *you* okay?" she finally asked.

I used my food as an excuse not to speak, chewing and nodding to show that I was fine.

"It's all right to have doubts, you know," she said.

I didn't want Baba to hear any of what I was going to say, because I was scared that he would think less of me. I looked over my shoulder carefully and muttered, "Where's Baba?"

Maman whispered, "He has gone out to see if he can get the tickets. Mamanjoon is in her room, listening to the radio."

"I'm scared, Maman," I confessed. "I don't want to leave without Baba."

Maman raised her eyebrows, as if to say that she felt exactly the same way. But I knew she would never go against Baba's wishes. Instead, she gave a little smile and said, "I know. I feel the same, but Baba is doing this because he loves you." She paused to see if I would protest, but I didn't. "It's not good for him either, you know. He'll really miss us, and he'll be lonely. He's doing this only because he thinks it's the best thing to do."

"And do you agree?" I asked. I did not want to cry. I had promised my father that I would be strong for my mother's sake. I could see that Maman was finding it difficult to answer the last question.

She looked at me as sternly as she could and said, "Yes. It is the best thing—for you, Abbas."

Did she really believe that, or did she just want to make me feel better?

"It will be really hard for us now, Abbas," she said in a crisp, controlled tone. "None of us will like what is about to happen, but we have to be there for Baba the way he is always here for us." Her voice was clear and certain, and it gave me confidence in what my father intended to do. "Now eat your breakfast, put your dishes in the sink, and go and have a shower."

"Do I have to?" I asked, putting on my cute face.

"No arguments. A shower, and then you're going to help me pack the things that need to be sold."

When I came out of the shower and passed Mamanjoon's room on the way to my own, I saw my mother's silhouette leaning toward my grandmother's bed. I was dripping wet, but curiosity got the better of me. Maman very rarely ventured into Mamanjoon's room, unless my grandmother was ill. The door was open a crack, and I put my face close to it to look inside. My mother was obviously distressed as she sat on the bed next to Mamanjoon, who lay there looking frail and troubled. The radio crackled on a stool next to her bed. Maman was talking to her in a pleading, desperate tone: "Please, you have to speak to him. We can't just up and leave Iran like this."

I was really taken aback. A few minutes ago, Maman had been backing all of my father's plans, and here she was trying to undo them. If Mamanjoon allied herself with my mother, then they would have a good chance of convincing my father to reverse his decision.

Mamanjoon took my mother's hand. "You have to go, my girl; there's no choice." Her voice was warm but firm.

But my mother did not seem ready to give up. "I choose to stay here with you and Karim. Abbas needs all his family."

But Mamanjoon could not be swayed.

"I know things are different now, but we must still understand where we stand in the bigger picture," Mamanjoon said. "In my day, we knew our duty, Marzieh. Even if my husband was wrong, I would still obey him."

My mother's response was cool. "I wish I could be as strong as you. You have so much to believe in, but I don't have that kind of regard for tradition." She paused and then added quickly, "I'm not sure I believe in anything anymore, other than my son and my husband."

Mamanjoon raised herself up from the bed and said, "Then you must obey your husband and save your child. That is the least you can do."

And that was the end of the conversation.

A little later, Baba ran in through the door, waving some papers about. He sat down with Maman and me around the kitchen table. He was slightly out of breath, with sweat dripping from his forehead. Maman poured him a cold glass of water, which he downed in one shot. Then he stood up and began to pace back and forth in the empty kitchen.

"It was almost impossible to get tickets to Istanbul," he said. "All the airlines are fully booked."

"So what happened?" Maman asked, obviously half hoping that we were not going anymore.

"I managed to get two, but the earliest tickets are not until a few weeks from now, right before Abbas's birthday." He stopped, waiting for a reaction.

"I see," were the only words Maman muttered after a long pause.

"And they were very expensive," he said, "because everyone wants to go to Istanbul at the moment." My father turned to my mother, who was staring blankly out of the window. "We have to sell everything, and I mean everything," he said.

"Yes, you said that before," Maman said in a flat tone.

"I had hoped we could spare a few things," Baba said, "but the tickets have set me back a small fortune."

We looked at each other silently. And then, Mamanjoon, like an old master of comic timing, chose this moment to hobble into the kitchen. Not noticing the tension in the air, she came over to Baba and kissed him on the forehead. Then she went over to the stove and looked at us.

"Tea, anyone?"

Maman smiled and gave a nervous little laugh. "Yes, please. We'll all have a glass, thank you."

"We will?" Baba mumbled, taken aback by Maman's response. "Yes, sure, thanks, Maman."

I guessed that my mother just wanted to keep Mamanjoon busy while we continued the conversation. If she were occupied, then she wouldn't ask questions.

I was really worried, but I was excited, too. I had never been involved in conversations as serious as this one before. I was not a participant, more an observer. Even so, I liked knowing what was going on.

Baba wiped his forehead and said, "You need to have as many dollars as we can get our hands on."

"I can get a job," I offered. I meant it, too. I had always wanted to make my own money. In fact, all my spare time went into working out how I was going to make more money than the week before.

Apart from the little jobs I got at the local stores, I would go to weddings with my parents and pick up coins and notes that were thrown at the bride and groom. I would collect and collect until my pockets were full and then ask my father to let me put my money in the car so that I could gather more. I would take it all home and count each rial and decide which bank account I wanted it to be deposited into by my father the next day. I was happy to remind my parents how good I was with money!

My father just stared at me. "No, Abbas. You can't be seen outside, remember?"

"Oh, yeah," I replied. Thinking back on it, my father was being very clever. He didn't use the fact that I was too young to work as a reason, but rather a technicality, which made me feel better about myself. Once again he fooled me, and he even brought a little smile to my mother's face.

The next morning, I thought I was going to get to sleep in, but my mother woke me at the usual time. She tapped me on my shoulder. "Come on, Abbas, time to get up."

"I'm not going to school, remember?" I muttered sleepily.

"Yes, but you have to help me pack things," she said. "Don't think you can get away without doing anything, you little monkey."

"Ahh," I groaned. "Do I have to?"

"Yes, you do. Now get up and get washed," she said firmly. "We've got a long day ahead of us." There was no point in arguing, and I knew it. So up I got, stumbled into the bathroom, and took a shower.

I couldn't believe how fast things were moving. I'd thought that because I wasn't going to school things would move more slowly, and I would be bored at home. Instead, the preparations kept me busy every minute, especially because of my father's thoroughness. He was trying to foresee almost every scenario that could possibly occur.

After breakfast, Baba asked me to empty my desk and put all the contents into a cardboard box. Off I went to my room, where I opened up the lid of the desk. It was surprising what

I had collected and forgotten about. A lot of the things inside were a mystery, and as I looked through them, it was like finding them all over again: pens I had thought were lost, stones I had picked up on travels with my parents, things I had made, and even photographs of my family.

It was strange. Suddenly I didn't want to empty my desk. The items I was putting in the box had been almost worthless to me the previous day, but now they seemed to be priceless. These were the only things that I possessed. It was a frightening and sad realization. I wasn't even sure what I would be allowed to keep in the end. Did they want my desk or my belongings? The only thing that I was going to fight for was my piggy bank. I treasured that the most.

After I had filled my box and my desk was empty, I filled another box with old clothes that were too small for me. I never cared about clothes, as I tended to rip most of them anyway. When I finished doing that, I strolled into my mother's room, where she was doing exactly what I had just done. Her face told me everything. It was the first time I saw her with an expression I could not only understand but also share, because she was going through all the feelings I'd gone through a few minutes earlier—only she seemed more upset. She had so many more memories. She was putting aside photographs that I had never seen before. These had been taken at the turn of the revolution and hidden away in cupboards.

I went to her and took a look over her shoulder. She was holding a picture of my father in a tuxedo, dancing with her in a chic red ball gown. I couldn't believe it. The photograph was like a Hollywood snapshot. She looked so beautiful, he looked so handsome, and they looked so happy. You could see how much in love they were by the way they stared into each other's eyes.

And I could see the sadness on my mother's face as she looked at the picture. I put my hand on her shoulder.

"I know how you feel, Maman. I didn't want to put my things in the boxes, either." I wasn't sure if that helped or not, but she nodded.

"Do you know where this was taken?"

I took a closer look, but I couldn't figure it out. I only knew that it looked very grand, like something out of a film. I put the photograph down and shrugged. My mother smiled and pointed to the floor.

"What?" I said. I didn't understand.

"Here," she said softly. "It was taken here. We were dancing in our living room."

"But it looks so different."

"We *were* different, my darling," she said as she brushed my hair away from my face with her hand. "We were rich. We were *very* rich." My mother was suddenly in another world as she placed herself back in that night. "You know the windows to the patio?"

"Yeah."

"They were opened out so that the living room spilled into the garden. We had a path that ran from the pool into the orchard and a marquee about thirty feet to the left of the pool. Can you imagine?" I shook my head in disbelief. "There was a band playing in the tent, and there were nearly three hundred people here that night."

"Three hundred?"

"Three hundred," she repeated, with a smile in her eyes. "Some very important people were here, Abbas."

"Who?" I demanded.

"Darius."

"What? The singer?" I shouted in excitement.

"Yes, the singer," she giggled. "Persia's foreign minister, at the time, was here too, and it was also the same night that your father proposed to me."

"Really?" I asked.

"Yes. He asked me in front of everyone. Then Darius sang to us while we danced."

"Wow," I could hardly believe it.

"It was one of the best nights of my life. That was what my life was like, and here these fools are, taking away what little I have left." Tears were rolling down her cheeks as she spoke. Without knowing it, I began to cry with my mother. It was not just from sadness but a new understanding of my mother's pain. I had never before really known what I had missed in my life and what should have been mine. Until that day. I didn't think of my father at the time, but now I know it must have been very hard for him, too, because he took great pride in seeing himself as the provider of the family. He always told me that, ultimately, you alone have to take responsibility for your situation. I can only imagine that by losing everything he must have lost face in his own eyes.

Over the next few weeks, my father gave my mother and me lessons about the dos and don'ts in Istanbul. He had spoken to his friends who either lived there or traveled there on business.

These lessons were pretty informal until a few days before we were to leave. My mother and I were sitting on the sofa in the living room. The room echoed with every little sound, as everything had been sold or was waiting in boxes to be sent off. My father was strolling up and down the room asking questions, and we answered like it was a quiz. He looked so worried. His shirt was wet with sweat. Little drops of it dripped from his head, and he was playing with his worry beads.

As he walked to the window, he stared out onto the main street where, in the distance, he could see people going in and out of shops. He turned back to us and said, "So then, what will you do for money when you get to Istanbul?"

"We'll swap only twenty dollars," my mother said.

"Why only twenty?"

I drawled out the answer in a way that showed I was bored: "Because we can get a better exchange rate on the black market."

"Don't act smart, Abbas," he snapped. "This is for your own good." I was shocked at his reaction and shut up quickly.

My mother reached out to comfort me silently while my father carried on.

"And then, what do you do after you've swapped your twenty dollars?" he asked in a softer voice. I think he could tell that he'd overreacted.

"We get a taxi and check out the hotels that your friend is going to suggest, and we choose the best one for us," my mother replied like a good student who has learned her lesson well.

"Yes, I'm calling my man in Istanbul tonight to get the names of the hotels," he said. "Remember that these hotels will be where a lot of Iranians congregate. Be polite and courteous to them, but not too friendly. If other Iranians are around, the locals won't try to rip you off, as it will seem like you know your way and that you know the rates." He paused as if he was trying to think of what else he could ask. It came to him. "What should you try to avoid?"

"We should use the buses rather than taxis, as they're a lot cheaper," I said quietly.

"Good. What else?"

"We should avoid going out at night," I said more confidently. I think my mother was bored with this now, but she kept quiet.

"And?"

"We shouldn't tell anyone how much money we have," I continued.

"That's very good, Abbas."

"Thank you, Baba."

"Try not to eat out, as it's too expensive . . ."

". . . and we don't know how long we're going to be there. I know, Baba."

"Right," he said. "Good boy."

"And, Baba?"

"Yes?"

"We shouldn't ask favors of anyone unless it is an emergency, because they will expect a bigger favor in return," I said, trying to show off my knowledge.

"Good lad, you're learning fast." As he said that, a blue van drove down our street and stopped outside the house. "Ah, here they are; the last of the boxes are going."

My father went to the door and opened it to let in two strangers. They were younger than my father, both with beards, wearing gray suits with shirts but no ties. They followed Baba into all the rooms, looked at what they could take, and then proceeded to choose what they wanted. They kept coming in and out of all the rooms and carrying away boxes, figurines, paintings, and pots and pans until they reached us in the living room. The television had already gone. The only thing that remained was the sofa we were sitting on.

Nobody had to say anything. My mother and I got up automatically. My mother shepherded me to the other side of the room as the men took the sofa to their van. I could see she was holding back her tears. She would not cry in front of strangers.

My father went outside to talk to them, and I went over to the window to see what was happening. They were obviously in an intense discussion about money. Baba looked like he was trying to control his emotions while fighting with all his might to get every rial that he could. Eventually, he gave in and they all walked back into the house. I could not see what else there was to sell. They went toward the bedrooms. Then they came out with my parents' bed. I could see my mother clench her fists. When she could not bear it anymore, she went out into the garden. Then Mamanjoon's bed came out. That really surprised me. If anyone needed a bed, it was Mamanjoon. She was praying as the men took her bed outside. She would pray five or six times a day, kneeling on her prayer mat, her *chador* wrapped securely around her head. It was strange to see the empty space where her bed had been and Mamanjoon on a prayer mat next to it.

My father took the money and came inside to be greeted only by me. He put his hand on my head and forced a fake grin as he said, "Mamanjoon's bed is more expensive than yours. I told her she could have yours."

"Sure, Baba, I like sleeping on the floor anyway," I said with my own fake grin, trying to make him feel better. "It's good for one's back."

"You're a good boy."

"Baba, come with me, will you?"

"Can it wait?" he asked.

"It's important," I said. "It will only take a few minutes." He nodded, and so I took him to the garden and through to the orchard. I found my special tree and began to dig under it.

"What are you doing?" he asked.

"Wait a second, Baba," I said. I dug hard until I got to the plastic bag that I had hidden. In it were my piggy bank and the account books for my three savings accounts. I handed them to him.

For a second Baba looked confused. Then he said, "Abbas, this is your money. I can't take—"

"Baba, I want to help."

He looked right into my eyes, grabbed me, and hugged me in a way he'd never done before. He then kissed me on the head and said, "Thank you, Abbas."

Three

A month of packing and planning, waiting and worrying rushed by. And then, finally, the day we were to leave arrived. Baba went out to change our money into dollars, and the house was quiet. He had left this until the last moment so that he could change all the money at one time; then he wouldn't have to pay the commission for exchanging it twice. Maman's bags and mine had been packed the previous night and stood by the door. I was dressed and ready to go. My footsteps echoed against the walls as I walked through all the rooms, looking for Maman and Mamanjoon.

As I entered the kitchen, I saw the two of them sitting on the floor with a plate and some dried bread in front of them. My mother gestured to me to sit next to them. Mamanjoon smiled. "Come over here, my darling. You should eat before leaving," she murmured. "It's going to be a long day."

I peered at the plate. "What is it?" I asked.

My mother tried to smile. "It's only fried onions with lavash, Abbas." She stopped to compose herself before continuing. "That's all we have left."

Fried onions! Since when had we started eating that? But I was hungry, and I could see that my mother was upset. So I sat down and took the smallest portion I could, putting the fried onions on a piece of the dry bread. My mother and Mamanjoon watched with great interest. After taking a small bite, I chewed very carefully, expecting the worst. To my surprise, it wasn't half bad, so I helped myself to more. I hadn't known fried onions and bread could taste this good.

"I knew you would like it," my mother said.

"So did I," I responded. She just smiled. She always knew what I was thinking.

While Mamanjoon was clearing the plates, the door opened. It was my father. He had a tight smile on his face.

"Time to go," he said. "Say goodbye to Mamanjoon, Abbas."

I walked over to Mamanjoon and stood in front of her. She held my cheeks with both her hands and kissed me. "I'll miss you, my darling. You take good care of yourself, and always remember that you are a Kazerooni. I've prayed for you, and I will continue to pray for you."

"Goodbye, Mamanjoon," I said. And then I began to sob.

"Come now, Abbas. Men don't cry; you know that," she said with a gentle smile. "You're a Kazerooni, remember?" She tidied my hair and took my hand. "Be strong, my boy. Be strong."

I tried to stop crying and waited for my mother to say goodbye to Mamanjoon. My grandmother hugged my mother tightly and whispered in her ear, "You're doing the right thing, my girl."

"Goodbye, Maman," my mother replied with tears in her eyes. Before I knew it, the three of us were in the car that my father had borrowed.

As my father pulled away, I looked at each of the houses on our street. So many memories flashed before my eyes: all of my soccer games, the times I had ripped my trousers, the fights I'd been in. I remembered how my friends Ali, Sourouh, Mehdi, and Farhad—the boys I played with on the streets—would come to my house and ask my mother if I could play. I remembered the bike rides, the games, the mischief we got into together, and the fun we had.

The car was going faster as we moved onto the main streets and eventually onto the motorway. No one had spoken since we had left. My mother and I were trying hard not to cry. Baba drove in auto-cruise. I could see his brain ticking as he tried to think of some last-minute advice to give us. He seemed desperate to keep calm. Out of the blue, he asked, "What's the capital of Turkey, Abbas?"

I thought for a minute and then guessed, "Istanbul."

My father gave my mother an amused look. Maman turned around and looked at me with a smile. I sighed with relief, as I thought I had got it right. Then my mother said, "It's Ankara, but it's a common mistake to make," as she jokingly slapped my father on the shoulder. "He's just trying to trick you."

That little incident was enough to take our minds away from the reality of the day, even if just for a few minutes. That is all I remember of the rest of the journey. I cannot remember the roads, what I saw, or what was said apart from that conversation. I know, however, that I looked out of the window for most of the ride, hoping it would never end. The longer it went on, the more hope I had that we would never arrive at Tehran Airport.

But then my father pulled up to the terminal. There was a deadly silence in the car. I could hear my mother breathing deeply, trying to control herself. My father sat staring through the windshield at the wall in front of him. I could hear him reaching for his worry beads in his left trouser pocket. Only about twenty seconds ticked past, but it felt like hours. Each of us was alone in that moment, and yet together one last time as a family. My father snapped us out of our reverie. "Come on, we've got to get you checked in."

I got out of the car slowly and went around to the trunk where my parents stood. My father pulled out our two suitcases while I reached in to get the smaller bags from the backseat. He looked at us, then picked up my bag and started to walk. My mother tried to carry her own bag, but I stopped her. "I'll take it, Maman."

"It's heavy," she said.

"I'll manage," I insisted.

She began to walk alongside my father. I hobbled behind them, struggling with the heavy suitcase. My father went through the main entrance, where thousands of people were sitting, eating, talking, and lining up. He stopped momentarily to look at a screen and then turned to my mother. "What's the flight number again?"

"IR391," I cut in.

My mother nodded to confirm. I could see that my quickness had put a smile on my father's face. All of a sudden, he had a spring in his step. He looked at the screen again and then began to lead us to a check-in desk about fifty yards away. Once again, I struggled behind with the suitcase. About twenty feet from the desk, my father stopped. He waited for me to catch up, took Maman's bag from me, and knelt down to my level.

"Abbas, you go over and sit on that seat," he said gently, "and save the two seats next to you for Maman and me. We'll go check in."

"Okay, Baba," I said and did as I was told. I was getting nervous. Would we be able to get on that flight? I watched as they joined the line. There were about four or five people ahead of them. My father leaned toward my mother and whispered something. My mother quickly checked her headscarf to make sure that her hair was not showing. At home she never bothered with the scarf, but in public it was compulsory. She often pushed the strict rules about dress to their limits, but this was not a good time or place to do that. I think my father was telling her this.

As the line moved forward, my parents looked as if they were chatting casually. Everything seemed to be running according to plan. I turned to scan the room: there were huge posters of Ayatollah Khomeini all over the airport. There were armed soldiers everywhere, some no older than sixteen or seventeen. I watched people saying their goodbyes.

I hadn't thought I'd taken my attention away from my parents for more than thirty seconds, but I obviously had, because as I looked back toward the check-in desk, I noticed they were at the head of the line. At first it all seemed normal, but then I saw that everything was not fine. My father and the man behind the desk were arguing. Baba looked shocked and angry. Both men kept looking at my mother. It was getting ugly when suddenly Baba stopped speaking. He put his hand out in acceptance of the situation and pulled my mother with him. She looked shaken. I wanted to go over and see what was happening, but I thought better of it.

I saw my father say something to my mother. She listened, looking more and more horrified with each word Baba spoke. Then she began to talk—in fact, she was almost shouting when my father shrieked for her to shut up. The entire terminal turned to see what was going on. My father whispered something to her and pointed to two seats, but not the ones near me. My mother was sobbing as she walked toward them.

I got up and started to walk over to my mother, but then I noticed my father staring at me. I stopped dead. He quietly motioned me back to my seat. I did what he wanted, but I could not take my eyes off my mother. She wouldn't look at me. I noticed my father walk briskly to the other side of the terminal until he reached a phone booth at the far end. He searched his pockets for change and his phone book. I was half watching him and half keeping an eye on my mother in case she made eye contact with me. She was hysterical. I had never seen her like this before.

My father looked around anxiously as he dialed a number and waited for a response. I could see he was desperate and trying hard not to show it. His eyes were scanning the terminal, making sure he was not being watched or overheard. Then he looked at me, and I knew he was talking about me.

He finished his conversation, slowly put the receiver down, and walked back toward me, every step deliberate, as if he was trying to buy time and think his plan through.

He sat next to me. He did not say anything. He sat there like a stranger. After crossing his legs, he got out his beads and sighed. I was too scared to say anything. Then he turned to me.

"They won't let your mother out," he said very calmly.

"What? Why's that?" I asked.

"Some technical issue. It's all rubbish," he said casually, as if talking to a friend about some small annoyance. "It's just a trick to try to keep you here."

"Oh," I said, confused. "So are we going home?"

"Well," he said, his voice almost a whisper, "I've been thinking. They're saying that they won't let your mother out, but they're not saying that they won't let *you* out."

"So?"

"Well, that means you can still go, Abbas."

"What, alone?" I asked. He must be joking.

"If you stay, you will probably go to war," he said. "I'm not saying you will die, but it's a strong possibility. However, if you go to Turkey, you'll have a chance at a life that I can't give you here in Iran. Obviously, if it doesn't work out, you can come back. There will be no shame in that. At least you will have tried."

He meant what he said. And while he was giving me the option to choose, in Persian culture, when your father gives you that kind of choice, you say yes. I had to go. I just nodded. I didn't have the strength to say yes out loud.

"Good lad," he said. "You're a Kazerooni through and through."

I smiled in order to stop myself from crying.

"Right," he said. "Because you're not even ten years old, you can't just get on a plane with no one to greet you at the other end. That's why I made that call. I have a friend in Istanbul who will pick you up, pretending to be your Uncle Farhad. I won't tell you his real name. It's better that way."

"How will I recognize him?" I asked.

"Good question," he said. "He will have a large card with your name on it. He'll say that he wrote it for the benefit of the flight attendant."

"Okay, so he'll pick me up for sure?"

"Yes. When you see him, run up to him as if you know him really well, and give him a kiss," he instructed.

"Then what?"

"He will take care of you. He owes me a favor from way back." He reached inside his jacket pocket and took out an envelope. He held on to it as he put it in my hands.

"Inside this envelope, Abbas," he said, "are one thousand seven hundred and one US dollars. Everything we have sold over the last month is here." He paused. "Look after it with your life, and it can give you a start not every child in this country gets."

"I will, Baba," I said, still trying not to cry. "I promise."

"Good boy," he said with a tender smile. "I'm very proud of you. You're very brave. Now sit here for a second while I try to check you in."

I watched him go over to the desk, which now had no line at all. This time he had no problem, but I could see that the man behind the desk was surprised as well as annoyed, because my clever father had trapped him in a loophole. It was so like my father to want to have the last word. And this time he did. He returned with a smile on his face, but as he reached me, he became serious again. "Remember all that I have taught you," he said. "Always think before you do or say anything."

"Yes, Baba."

"And call me as soon as you reach Istanbul, okay?"

"I will."

"Now is the time you have to be a man, my son," he said. "Go and say goodbye to your mother, but please do not cry, as she's already very upset."

"Okay," I said, trying to hold back all my feelings. This was no ordinary goodbye. My mother was the person I loved most in the world. I walked over to where she sat crying.

"I have to go now, Maman," I said. I stood next to her stiffly, my eyes filled with tears, and all I was thinking about was trying to stop them from rolling down my cheeks. "Goodbye, Maman."

My mother held me so tightly that I could barely breathe. She was weeping, and I felt guilty for not showing my feelings.

"Goodbye, my darling," she said. "I love you so much . . . I love you more than anything in this world, Abbas. You know that, right?"

I just nodded.

"I'm so sorry you're going alone, but I promise to join you as soon as I can. I'll try to be there for your birthday in a week."

"Come on, Abs. We've got to get you through the gate," my father said from a distance.

"Now you look after yourself," were my mother's last words. As I walked away from her, I saw her fall to her knees, crying inconsolably. At the gate, when the flight attendant was about to take me away, my father offered his hand for me to shake. His grip was firm. He held my hand in his while he said, "Good luck, Son." And then, "Have a good trip."

I couldn't bear to look back as I walked away from the gate, tears rolling down my face.

I cannot remember very much about that flight. I sat in my seat and stared out the window, hoping I would get one last look at my parents before taking off. Then I cried myself to sleep even before the plane took off. Before I knew it, I was landing in Istanbul, where it was already night.

I waited until the flight attendant came to get me. I don't remember what we talked about on our brief walk to the arrivals lounge, but I know that I only gave her yes and no answers. I was more worried about seeing my name on the card and acting in a way that wouldn't give the game away. We had cut ahead of all the lines, and suddenly we were at the lounge. My eyes were working overtime. In a panic, I saw that there were many signs, with many different names. Then in the back, I spotted a tall man with a dark beard and mustache who was obviously Iranian. He was wearing a black shirt and black trousers and had sunglasses on, even though it was night.

As soon as I saw him holding my name up, I made a dash for him. I think he was surprised when I jumped up, hugged him, and gave him the two traditional Iranian kisses, saying, "Hey, Uncle Farhad, how are you?"

Before he could reply, the flight attendant appeared with her papers.

"Farhad Kazerooni?" she asked with a smile.

"That's me," he responded with a fake smile. He took the papers from her and signed them, then watched her leave. Eventually, he noticed me looking up at him, waiting for instructions.

"Go and swap twenty dollars at the foreign exchange office," he ordered.

"But my father said that I should swap money on the black market because I'll get a better rate," I said hesitantly.

"Did he now?" the man said with an arrogant smile. "Well, he's right, but what exactly does he expect you to use to pay for the taxi?"

As I walked to the foreign exchange office, I was thinking about what he had said. Why would I need a taxi, now that Maman wasn't with me as planned? Hadn't Baba said this man would look after me? I didn't want to argue, though, so I put twenty dollars on the counter, and the lady gave me the equivalent amount in Turkish lira. I walked slowly back to the man and waited to see what he would do next.

"Right. Here's a list of the cheapest hotels in Istanbul that you'll be safe at," he said. "Only Iranians stay at these hotels, and everyone speaks Farsi. The taxi line is over there. Now, my number is at the bottom of the piece of paper, but do not call it. I repeat, do not call it, unless it's a matter of life and death. Do you understand?"

"Yes," I replied, hardly believing what I was hearing.

"Good, well, off you go then," he said with another phony smile.

"But my father said that you'd look after me."

"Your father says many things. I don't have time to stay here and entertain you," he snapped. "Now, if you won't go, I will."

The man walked off into the crowd, and before I knew it, he'd disappeared. There I was with my suitcase, in the middle of Istanbul Airport. Alone. I didn't even realize I was crying until I saw the tears hit my shoes. Outside it was dark. Night. I was nine years old and by myself in a foreign land. I didn't even speak the language.

Quite simply, I was terrified.

ISTANBUL

FOUR

What should I do? I didn't trust anyone. As much as I wanted to stop crying, I couldn't. I resigned myself to the fact that my adventure had come to an abrupt end. I turned around to go back to the Iran Air counter to get a flight back to Tehran somehow. There was only one man there. He had a sharp, mean face with a pointy nose and a long beard. I decided against it.

As I stood helplessly looking around, a man brushed past me, pushing me off balance and shouting at me in a foreign language. I realized that I was standing right in the middle of a busy airport in everyone's way. Someone was bound to notice and start questioning me. I touched my pockets to make sure my passport and money were still there. My father had taught me about pickpockets.

I struggled with my suitcase, pulling it to one side where there were many seats, some with people sleeping on them. Children no younger than me were doing what kids do—annoying their parents, crying at the smallest things. I was not ready to be where I was, on my own, having to make the decisions that I guessed I would have to make. What was I going to do? If I went back, my father would definitely be disappointed in me, and the more I thought about it, the more unrealistic that idea felt.

I was left with two options. I would either have to ask for help or make a decision on my own. I knew that I could not keep crying—no one cared anyway—so I made my very first major decision. Slowly, I picked myself up and pulled my bags to the large doors near the taxi line. I observed what others did: they approached the taxis and simply got into them. Even this seemed impossible at the time. How could I get into a taxi with a strange person? What if he robbed me of all I had?

All these thoughts were whirling in my head when I heard, "Taxi?" I saw a tall, thin man with salt-and-pepper curly hair looking at me. He was dressed in an old checked shirt and beige trousers. His once-black shoes were worn to a scruffy gray. But his face was clean-shaven, and he had a friendly smile.

"Taxi?" he asked again.

I nodded .

"Iranian?" he asked in Farsi.

"Yes," I said.

"Maman . . . eh . . . Baba . . . where?" he asked in broken Farsi.

"Not here." I kept it short on purpose. I did not want to make myself more vulnerable than I already was.

"Okay," he said. "Where you go?"

I looked at him one more time before committing myself fully. Then I reached into my denim pocket for the scrunched-up list that Farhad had given me. I slowly brought it out and handed it to him. The taxi driver smiled to himself as soon as he saw the list. He was about to pick up my suitcase when I grabbed it. I was paranoid that everyone was out to take advantage of me. The taxi driver immediately withdrew his hand from the handle and backed away with a smile.

"It's all right . . . I help . . . only help."

"I'm okay."

"Fine," he said with a smile. "Follow me . . . taxi there." I followed him with the suitcase, trying not to let him see that it was too heavy for me. I was struggling to lift it into the trunk of the taxi when he reached down to help me. This time I let him. He smiled at me, showing his pleasure at my small gesture of trust. I pretended it was nothing and continued with the task at hand. My instincts were telling me that this was a good man, but I had to be sure.

In silence, I climbed into the backseat, and the driver shut the door after me. The inside of the taxi smelled of stale tobacco and sweat. A fine leopard-skin-print sheet, with holes and stains indicating its age, covered the backseat. In the front, the rear-view mirror had worry beads hanging from it. The driver's seat was covered with a brightly colored sheet. The man jumped in, then turned to me and smiled. He began to pull away from the curb, sticking his head out of the window, waving and shouting in order to get out of his spot and onto the main road. He appeared to be a seasoned professional, and from his gestures and posture, he seemed at home behind the steering wheel. We both sat in silence as he drove out of the airport.

I was not sure if he knew where he was taking me, and if he had understood exactly what I wanted, but I dared not speak. Eventually, I built up the courage to say something, but just then the driver looked at me in the rear-view mirror and said, "What is your name?"

"Abbas," I answered.

"Meeting you nice, Mr. Abbas. My name . . . Ahmed." He chose his words carefully. "We go to . . . er . . . different hotels . . . check price, yes?"

"Yes." How did he know this? I was on my guard. I wanted to look out of the window to see what Istanbul had in store for me, but I had to concentrate on what he was saying. I couldn't let him cheat me.

"I speak good Farsi, yes?"

I nodded. I had wondered how he was able to speak Farsi.

"Er . . . how you say . . . many customers are Iranian."

I had heard this from my father, that there were many Iranians in Istanbul. "How many?" I inquired.

"They say about half to one million."

"A million?"

"Yes," Ahmed replied with a wry smile.

"That *is* a lot." I could not believe it.

I suddenly realized that I was happily talking to Ahmed. I had let my guard down too easily and was angry with myself for trusting someone so quickly.

"That is how I know what you want," he continued, waiting for a response. He did not get one, and so he added, "The hotels . . . most Iranians come with similar list . . . these hotels are known in Istanbul for Iranian guests. Taxi drivers know them very good. We go look. Ahmed help find good deal, yes?"

"Thank you," I said. There was a long silence as Ahmed drove for another ten minutes. My mind was drifting to the image of my mother crying at the airport and falling to her knees. How could I have left her?

The thought of her finding out how Farhad had deserted me at the airport in Istanbul scared me. I knew that she would be beside herself with worry. She would find out soon enough, but how was I to ease the news?

Ahmed reached toward his glove compartment. This brought me out of my reverie, and I jumped at his move. What was he was looking for? It could be anything from a toothpick to a gun. My heart was racing.

Then he turned around with a big smile and handed me a photograph.

"My family," he said proudly. "They live in village far away. My son next to me . . . he . . . your age."

I could see what he was trying to do, and it made me feel a little better. I liked the fact that he had a son. It seemed less likely that he was going to harm me. For another ten minutes, I sat nervously in the back of the taxi listening to Ahmed give me a tour of Istanbul in his pidgin Farsi. Usually, I would have found it highly entertaining, but at the time, my mind was focused on what the hotels would be like and how they would react to a nine-year-old looking for a room all by himself.

Just then, Ahmed took a sharp left turn from one of the main streets onto a side road. It was not lit. The old buildings on either side of the road loomed up before us. I felt my stomach churn. Had I misjudged Ahmed? My father had told me terrible stories of children being killed for their organs and other horrible scenarios to make me aware of the dangers that I might face.

By the time I had built up the courage to say something, Ahmed took another quick turn, this time to the right. As I was jolted out of my seat, I noticed a distant lit-up building in the otherwise dark shadows of the run-down road. Graffiti covered the walls and random drunk figures hobbled along the pavement.

Ahmed stopped the car next to the building. A small neon sign indicated that it was a hotel. Ahmed looked at me but said nothing. I stared at him for an awkward three or four seconds. Then he raised his hand gently to indicate that I should go in if I wanted to check the prices. I did not want to show how scared I was, and so I decided to go for it. I opened the door gently and then looked back at Ahmed.

"I wait here . . . yes?" he said gently.

Then I thought about my things. My suitcase was in the trunk of the taxi, and my other bag was in the back with me. I could not take the bags in—but then again, the most important things like my money and my passport were on me. I decided to risk it. I nodded to Ahmed that I would be back soon. I got out of the taxi, and the pungent smell of wet coal on the road hit me as I slowly climbed the narrow stairs to the hotel's makeshift lobby. I opened the door to find a smoke-filled room with a small reception area. Tacky plastic plants were scattered around the room. The windows were so dirty that I could not see outside.

A sweaty, unshaven man sat behind the counter. He wore a thin cotton shirt with old trousers. His bare feet were perched on the desk. The smell of stale smoke and food—stale kebab—filled the air. It was beginning to make me feel sick.

I looked at the man but got no reaction. I looked again, and suddenly, in a sharp and abrupt tone, he said something in Turkish.

"I don't understand Turkish," I said. "Do you . . ."

"Ah, Iranian, yes?" he grinned. He took a deep puff of his cigarette as I nodded. "It's okay. I speak Farsi," he said, as if he could already hear the *ching-ching* of his cash register in his head.

"How much is it for a single room?" I asked.

He stubbed out his cigarette and leaped to his feet, towering over me. For the first time, I saw his sharp, stained, revolting teeth. "How long are you staying?"

"I don't know," I said.

"I see," he said with a sly smile. "Well, I can't give you price for a single room. You share with your mother, yes?"

"No, it's just me," I said quickly. I was thinking about the meter running in the waiting taxi.

"Okay," he murmured as he lit another cigarette. "I can give you good price of twelve thousand lira a night."

I was about to respond when I heard, "Give boy break . . . this no Hilton, my friend."

It was Ahmed. He was standing at the lobby door. He gave me a little wave to indicate that it was going to be all right.

"Who are you?" the man asked, glancing at me to see if we were together.

"A friend," Ahmed responded coolly. "Now you give good price, or we go other hotel."

The man sat down on his chair and mumbled something in Turkish at Ahmed, which I later found out to be an offer of nine thousand lira a night.

"Abbas," Ahmed said with a wry smile, "we look . . . different hotel, my friend."

He guided me out of the hotel, and I felt relieved. I had already made a good friend. Distracted, I misjudged the steps and fell all the way to the bottom. I was in pain, but there was no way I was going to cry. I stood up quickly and laughed at myself the way one does in that kind of situation. However, my back was really hurting. I opened the taxi door and got in.

I was glad to be out of that hotel and even happier to cushion my back.

It was already late at night in Istanbul. I was worried about what my parents would be thinking. I had promised to call as soon as I reached Farhad's house.

"Next hotel," Ahmed said, "is very near."

"Okay," I responded. I was tired, but I suspected that we would need to see at least five or six more hotels before I could decide.

Ahmed was driving down the backstreets of the European side of the city. It was totally dark except for the lights of the cars on the roads. By now, I trusted him totally. He could have taken me anywhere, and I would not have questioned him. We had traveled for only a few more minutes when Ahmed took one of his customary snappy turns onto a long, straight road. The road was not well lit, but I could see the flashing lights of police cars and bright torches in the distance. Ahmed immediately slowed down and rolled toward the light. Obviously, the hotel was in that direction. As we came closer, it became clear that the police activity was right outside the hotel. The police had taped off the area. A policeman waved Ahmed past the tape, and I couldn't help but look.

Behind him lay a man, bleeding and motionless. His face was sliced, and he looked like he had been beaten and stabbed. People were peeking out of the lobby window. I saw a child crying as his mother tried to comfort him.

I felt sick. I had been scared and nervous, but now my nerves were totally frayed. I just wanted to be with Baba and Maman. I was sweating heavily, and yet I was cold. I wiped my forehead and tried hard to resist bursting into tears.

As the taxi pulled away from the site, Ahmed turned around and looked at me. "We go different hotel, yes?"

"Yes," I murmured quietly. I could not even look at him for fear of crying.

"Next hotel far, but Ahmed get there fast," he said with a smile, trying to make me feel better.

We left the screechy ambulance sirens behind and drove for another fifteen or twenty minutes, with Ahmed going through his repertoire of jokes in Farsi, trying to cheer me up. However, nothing was going to get the image of that bleeding corpse out of my mind. Eventually, Ahmed gave up and we drove in silence.

I kept my head down. I was afraid of what I might see. This was not quite the introduction I had expected to this ancient and famous city. Even so, I had no choice but to look up when I felt the car come to a halt. I saw a disappointed expression on Ahmed's face. He pointed out of his window.

I had no idea where we were. The street looked as filthy as the last one. I peered out at the hotel he had brought me to, and I saw a small neon sign flashing "Full" in the window. I let out a sigh.

"Big sigh for little man," Ahmed said with a grin. I just

shrugged, not knowing when—or if—my luck with hotels was going to change.

"Next?"

I nodded. I took another peek at my watch. It was well past midnight, which meant that it was even later in Iran. I imagined my parents must have been worried, as they had heard nothing from me since I had left. I expected they would ask me to return as soon as they heard what had happened to me here. Maybe we could buy back everything we had sold and have our old life back. At that moment, nothing seemed more pleasing to me.

Considering the night I had just experienced, it was about time that I had some good luck. However, this was Istanbul and I was already beginning to discover that you never knew when you'd be disappointed.

Finally, we came to another hotel on a dark road. It seemed identical to all the others we had tried. It was hard to see what this hotel was really like, as it, too, was badly lit. But it had a better feel to it than the previous stops. And while this road had the same psychological hurdles—graffiti on its walls and drunks wandering home—from the start, it felt right.

Ahmed stopped the car, and we both got out without looking at each other. I was glad he was with me. I climbed the three or four steps to the hotel. Again, the lobby was small and dingy, but cleaner than that of the first hotel. The few plants that decorated the lobby were real. They were in desperate need of watering, but at least they were not fake, plastic ones.

The reception area was empty. I rang the small bell on the desk. I could barely see the other side of the counter. I had just put the bell back when a tall, thin man came out of what looked like a small kitchen. He seemed tired and had not shaved that day, but he had friendly eyes. He was wearing a cheap beige suit and a sweat-stained shirt. His tie was halfway down his neck, and his shoes were old, though polished clean. He managed a small smile.

"Hello," he said in a surprisingly deep voice. "How can I help you?" At least I presumed that is what he said. He was speaking in Turkish, but I think he knew that I was Persian.

"Do you speak—"

"Farsi? Of course I do. In fact, I speak it very well." His words were spoken more in humor than arrogance.

"Do you have any single rooms available?"

"Single?" he asked as he looked at Ahmed.

Ahmed returned the glance. "He's not with me," he said. "I'm just a friend."

"I see," the receptionist said. "Well, in that case, yes, I do. However, I need money in advance. Too many of you Persians leave without settling the bill."

"Okay," I said, "but how much per night?"

"Eight thousand five hundred lira, and if you stay more than two weeks, it goes down to eight thousand."

"How about six and a half and six thousand?" Ahmed asked.

The receptionist and Ahmed exchanged a few words in Turkish. Then the man looked at me and said, "Okay, but how do I know if you have any money?"

I didn't know what to do, and so I looked at Ahmed. He nodded, and taking the cue, I nodded back at the man. Nothing happened. The receptionist kept looking at me as if he expected me to do something. When he realized that I had not caught on, he said, "You have to pay week by week—in advance."

I looked at Ahmed again, not knowing if this was the standard procedure.

"It is best deal you get, Little Man," he said. "It late, and I have to go see family now. I go get bags."

So I dug into my pockets, reaching for the bundle of dollars, and with my fingers, I wiggled one bill away from the rest of the pile. Luckily for me, it was a fifty. I held it out, and the receptionist's eyes immediately lit up. I looked at him and said, "Keep this until tomorrow, when I will give you lira. Then you give me back my dollars."

"That is fair."

I turned to Ahmed and said, "How much for you?"

"It is okay, Little Man. You need lots help, and I want to help little," he said.

The receptionist was desperately trying to act like he was not listening, but he was all ears.

"No, Ahmed, you take some money," I said.

Ahmed could see that I was serious and wanted to give him something. "How about five hundred lira?"

I reached into my pocket, took out fifty cents—about five hundred lira—and handed it to him. He waved at me and turned to go.

"Ahmed?"

He turned once again to face me. "Yes?"

"I just wanted to say . . . well . . ."

"I know, Little Man, I know," he said with a dignified smile. "It has been pleasure for Ahmed."

As I waited, he carried my bags into the lobby. Then, as I watched through the lobby window, his taxi disappeared into the dark. I thanked God that I had met him that night.

I turned from the window to see the receptionist smiling at me from behind his desk. "Ah, yes, let me show you to your room," he said. "You're on the second floor."

"Thank you."

"By the way, my name is Murat."

He looked a little mad, but I instinctively felt he was a good man. He didn't look crazy in the sense that he could kill me or anything like that, but as if he lived in his own little world. That made me like him. I was living pretty much in my own little world, too.

FIVE

Murat led me up some dark, damp stairs covered in a dirty green carpet. He was stocky, with short dark hair and deep-set brown eyes, and while he wasn't a huge man, he had a presence that couldn't be ignored. As I followed him, I noticed his slow, deliberate steps. We walked through a dim corridor to Room 201, which was to be my home for the foreseeable future. He turned the key and opened the door only slightly, so that I could not see inside. "Goodnight," he said. "Abbas, is it?"

"Yes," I replied. "Goodnight, Murat." I heard him whistle to himself as he walked away. I almost didn't dare open the door, but I was tired. I lifted my bags and pushed the door with my foot. It opened to reveal a tiny room with a big bed in the center. It was covered with a thick sheet and flanked by bedside tables on either side. The bed took up almost all the space. There was a banged-up old cupboard with a sliding door at its foot. A small window, its frame covered in flaky blackish-green mold, looked out on the street. And that was it.

I felt a chill. I had only seen rooms like this in movies. A cockroach to the left of the bed, next to a door, caught my attention. I didn't dare open that door yet. I patted the sheets. They were clammy. There were stains all over them, including several crimson stains, which made me feel queasy. I opened the door to the left of the bed and found a bathroom. Good thing I did, because I was sick and threw up until I had nothing left inside me. How I wished my mother were there, rubbing my back and trying to make me feel better!

Finally, I stopped throwing up and raised my head to take a look around me. The bathroom was filthy. The red tile was mixed with patches of yellow paint covering random areas on the walls. A shower hung above me. There was a huge drain in the center of the slightly sloping floor, smudged with stains. Then I saw a sharp object poking through the drain. It looked like a used syringe, which I knew was bad news. I went to the trash basket and took out the plastic liner. I used it as a glove, making sure the needle did not come into contact with my skin. Very carefully, I picked it up and turned the liner inside out so that the needle was at the bottom of the bin. After that, I washed my hands for what seemed like forever, soaping my arms up to the elbows like a surgeon, while I watched more cockroaches scuttling around the edges of the bathroom.

How was I going to cope with all this? I kept finding myself close to tears, faced with having to solve one problem after another on an endless list.

My first night in Istanbul seemed like it was never going to end.

I sat on the bed to think about my next move. I opened my suitcase and was putting all my clothes on the bed in small piles—socks, trousers, jeans, T-shirts, shirts, sweaters—when I heard a loud noise.

Someone was shouting in the street. I dared myself to creep to the window and take a peek. It was dark, and all I could make out was a man stumbling around with what seemed like blood all over his face. He was shouting like a wild animal. He kept falling over, but when he found anything on the street, like bottles or cans or stones, he would pick them up and throw them at the buildings.

Eventually, he threw a stone through a glass window, and within seconds a light came on. A man leaned out and started to shout in Turkish. Then he disappeared only to reappear with a big stick. He ran after the man in the street and began to beat him. I could hear every thud. Once again, I realized how vulnerable I was in this strange place. How I wished my father—

And there it was. I suddenly remembered that I had not called my parents.

My watch read 3 a.m. It must have been dawn in Tehran. Honestly, I did not want to leave my room, but the telephone was downstairs. I locked the door behind me and began to make my way slowly along the dark corridor. Then I ran down the two flights of stairs as quickly as I could.

Murat was half-asleep. "Something wrong?" he asked.

"No, I just need to . . ."

"Did you see what happened outside?"

"No," I said, pretending all was well. I did not want to talk about it. "I just want to use the telephone," I said.

"Yes, of course," he said, a little distracted. "You give me the number and then when I connect, you pick up the phone in one of those." He pointed to three little cubicles at the far end of the small lobby.

"Okay," I replied. "Can they call me, too?"

"Yes."

"May I have the number for the hotel, please?"

"Sure." As he pulled out a card with the hotel's details, he said, "Do you still want to make a call?"

"Yes," I said. He looked at me, and I thought he was trying to figure out if I had been crying. I didn't think he could tell, as I had washed my face and I was acting a lot more confident that I actually felt.

He handed me a piece of paper and a pen, and I wrote down my home number for him.

I looked at my watch again as Murat dialed. What should I tell Baba, and what should I omit? I was sure that if I told him half of what had happened in Istanbul, he'd have me on the first plane home. There was no need to worry him more than necessary. I got my plan together.

Murat started to wave, and I could hear him saying, "I have

an international call for you from Istanbul." The phone in the first cubicle started to ring. I took a deep breath.

"Hello?" I said, hoping for a friendly voice.

"Abbas, is that you?" I heard my father say. I could hear both the anger and concern in his voice.

"Yes, Baba, it's me," I said softly.

"Where have you been? Why didn't you—"

"Baba," I screamed, "take down this number, and call me back at my hotel."

"Hotel? What hotel?" he demanded.

"Baba, call me back and I'll tell you." I could not believe that I had spoken to my father like that. Suddenly, I felt a rush of power, and it felt good. I gave him the number and put the phone down. I felt a little less worried about talking to him now, but I still expected a bombardment of questions. The inquisition was about to commence.

I waited in the cubicle. Sure enough, within minutes the phone rang, and even before either of us spoke, I could feel the intensity of my father's fury.

"Hello?"

"Abbas? Why are you in a hotel?" he asked. "What happened to the man who was supposed to pick you up?"

"Once I found him, he told me to swap twenty dollars at the bank. I told him you'd told me not to, but he insisted."

"Okay," he said, sounding curious. "Then what happened?"

"Well, I thought he was going to take me with him as you

had said he would, but instead he just gave me a list of hotels and told me where I could find a taxi."

I could feel my father getting angrier as the silence grew, so I decided to continue with my account. "I didn't know what to do, Baba. If I had asked for help at the airport, I was sure they'd send me back."

"So what did you do?"

I heard my mother's sweet voice in the background. "Don't be so hard on the boy. He's trying his best. Is he all right?"

"Just let me deal with this, Marzieh, will you?"

"Baba, is that Maman? Can I speak to her?"

"No, you can't," my father retorted. "You just tell me what happened next."

"Well, I went and found a taxi and started to look at prices from the list that the man gave me."

"That idiot!" he shouted. "If I get my hands on him—"

"Karim," my mother interrupted.

"So what are these hotels like, Abbas?"

"They're okay, Baba," I said, trying to sound like I meant what I was saying, "and I got a good rate, I think. The taxi driver helped me."

"What taxi driver?"

"The one who drove me from hotel to hotel."

"He's gone, right?"

"Yes, Baba, he's gone," I said firmly.

"So how much is the hotel?"

I hesitated for a while, as I did not know if my deal was good or not. I crossed my fingers.

"Six thousand five hundred lira a night for the first two weeks and then six thousand lira a night after that."

There was a pause. I could imagine my father running the numbers in his head. "That's not bad, Abs."

Music to my ears! From my father, that was a compliment.

"What should I do next, Baba?" There was silence; then I heard my parents arguing.

"Just let me speak to him for a few seconds, Karim," I heard my mother beg. "Please?"

"The boy's traumatized. I don't need him to be more upset."

"He's my son, too," she said, her voice rising. "Let me speak to him now."

"Not until you're calm, woman."

"I *am* calm," she screamed. "Who do you think you are?"

"Baba," I said quietly, but there was no response as they continued to argue. "Baba!" I called louder.

"What?" he snapped.

"Why can't I speak to Maman?"

"Because you will upset each other."

"Well, I am going to see you soon anyway, right?"

There was a pause. I was convinced he was going to tell me how to get back to Iran. However, the longer the silence stretched, the more I worried that this might not happen.

"Baba?"

"Yes?"

"I am coming home, right?"

"I don't think you should, Abs," he said softly.

My worst nightmare had come true. I could not believe that my father was going to let me—no, *make* me—stay in this hell.

I felt tears roll down my cheeks. I did not want my father to know that I was crying, so I didn't speak. I think he was trying to choose his words carefully in order to make me feel better. However, at that moment, I needed more than a few carefully chosen words. I needed more confidence, I needed to be older, and most of all I needed my parents.

Alternatively, I needed a miracle.

"Abs?" he said. "You still there?"

"Yes," I murmured.

"You're going to have to be strong now, Abs," he said. "You're going to have to be a man."

What could I possibly say to this? I could not tell him that I couldn't cope. I didn't want him to be disappointed in me. All my life he had told me how much he expected of me. So I held my tongue, though deep down I did not know how I was going to survive. I did not know what to do, or who to trust, and from what I had seen that night, I did not know if I was going to live to see another day.

"Abs?"

"Yes?"

"You've already shown me you can handle yourself like an adult," he said.

I bit my tongue. I was scared to death, and all I wanted was to have my mother hold me.

"You got a taxi all the way from the airport and looked around a strange city for a good hotel. It is a really good hotel, right?"

"Er . . . I guess," I said.

"And it's in a good area, right?"

"Yes," I said, resigning myself to lying. It was not worth both of us feeling bad. I understood that my father carried the responsibility for my safety solely on his shoulders. My mother had wanted no part in this. He probably felt guilty for sending me off alone. I didn't want to add to his guilt.

"Yes," my father continued, "if you can get a taxi in Istanbul, go around and compare rates, and find a good hotel all by yourself, then there's no reason why you can't do everything else by yourself, is there?" I couldn't bring myself to answer him. "Is there? Abs?"

"No, Baba."

"Good, then, it's settled."

I wasn't sure who he was trying to fool.

"Baba?"

"Yes?" he said.

"What exactly do I have to do?" I asked.

"Well, you have to get to the British Embassy somehow," he said, thinking quickly. "There you have to try to get a visa."

"I have to exchange money first, Baba, to pay for the hotel," I said. "They want payment weekly, in advance, and I've left a fifty-dollar deposit until I get lira. Then I'll get my fifty back."

"Right, then that's what you have to do," he said, "but don't—"

"I know, don't swap it at the bank," I said. "I'll find a black-market dealer like you told me to."

"Good lad," he said, getting excited again. "Good lad. I told you that you could do it. Just ask someone Persian to-morrow where they swap their money, and then go and get it from the same place. You can bet that they would've found the best deal."

"Okay," I said, not totally convinced, "and what shall I do at the embassy?"

"Ah, yes," he said. "At the embassy, you'll find it a little difficult because they don't speak Farsi. They only speak Turkish and English."

"So what shall I do, Baba?"

"I'm guessing that there will be some Iranians there. Ask one of them to help. Never be shy to ask for help; just choose who you ask carefully, as they may try to take advantage of you."

"How do I know who to choose?" I asked.

"That's a good question, Son," he said. "I'm still trying to work that one out for myself. It's about knowing who you can trust or not trust. Some people have it in them to know and some don't. It's like a sixth sense, Abs. We'll soon see if you have it or not . . . but I think you do."

"I do?"

"I think so, Son," he said. "I think so."

For the first time during the conversation, I felt a little better. The fact that my father thought I had something that most people don't have was great.

"So if I get someone to help me, Baba," I inquired, "what do I tell them at the embassy?"

"The truth, Abs," he said firmly. "Always tell them the truth, because if you don't, they'll find out, and you'll never get to England."

"Okay."

"Tell them that you had to leave to avoid having to go to war. Tell them that your father believed that the best thing for a child of your age is education, and that you were not going to be allowed to get it in your own country. Tell them that the regime was so determined to drag you into the war that they stopped your parents from leaving with you. Tell them that you want to go to England to stay with your cousin, Mehdi, who has lived there for fourteen years and has British citizenship. He has agreed to be your guardian. He is a chef, if they need to know that. They will need documentation. Write down what they ask for, and I will call you around nine o'clock your time tomorrow night. You can tell me what documentation is needed, and I'll get it to you as fast as I can. Okay?"

It seemed so simple to him, but that was a lot of information for me. I was scared that I would get it all wrong.

"Okay," I said.

"Abs?"

"Yes, Baba?"

"Be careful, my boy. Don't leave the hotel at night."

"I wasn't going to," I said. I couldn't tell him that, having seen what I had, I'd prefer to avoid leaving the hotel even during the day!

"Good boy," he said.

"Baba?" I said gently.

"Yes, Abs?"

"Can I speak to Maman, please?"

"Not tonight, Son," he responded. I knew he had sensed the desperation in my voice, and still he had said no. "Maybe tomorrow." I had no energy to argue with him, but I missed my mother more than anything else. "Now go to bed, Abs," he ordered. "You must be tired."

"Yes, I am. Say goodnight to Maman for me."

"I will."

"Goodnight, Baba."

"Goodnight, Son," he said. "Oh, Abs?"

"Yes?"

"We're proud of you, Son."

I put the phone down, unable to breathe. I was glad that it was late, as I didn't want anyone to see me like this. I calmed myself, then opened the cubicle door, crept past reception, and ran up the stairs.

I opened the door to my room to see my clothes still on the bed. I slowly started to put them away. All I could think about was finding somewhere to swap money the next day and not getting ripped off, then finding the embassy, and trying to find someone to help me communicate there. It was all too much.

I turned off the light and crept to the side of the bed, but I could not force myself to lie on it. I switched on the light again, and then edged my way onto the bed. It was cold and the sheets were damp. A small, chilly draft was whistling through the gaps in the window. Every little noise was apparent to me. The flapping of the curtains was making me feel as though I was being watched. Every shadow in the room looked like some enormous monster. I was so tired, but I did not want to sleep, for fear that I would not wake again.

For the first time that night, my sobbing had a sound. I was hungry, I was thirsty, and, most of all, I was homesick. The night just didn't want to end, and yet after minutes of crying—minutes that seemed like hours—I drifted into sleep.

Six

I remember waking up the first morning in Istanbul in a daze. I was hoping the previous night had been a dream, but it hadn't. It wasn't even light yet, but the noises of early morning had woken me up.

I did not want to get out of bed. If I just stayed there, maybe everything would get better. I knew that was wishful thinking, so I dared myself to look outside. After what I had seen the night before, it was not such an easy thing to do. I crept out of bed, made my way to the side of the window, and gently lifted the edge of the curtain. This way, I could look out and not be seen—at least that was what I hoped.

My first impressions were not great. The street looked even dirtier in the daylight. There seemed to be litter everywhere, and the pungent smell of damp coal and rubbish mixed together was overpowering.

The few people who were up that early were all going about their business, ignoring one another. Some of them seemed to be returning home from the night before. The street and the buildings looked gloomy, gray, and cold, despite the fine morning. I could not help but have a feeling of foreboding.

I inched away from the window and went into the bathroom. Usually, my mother would have to remind me to bathe in the morning, but that day I felt so dirty from the night before that I couldn't wait to have a shower.

The bathroom door would not lock however hard I tried. I did not feel safe, even within my room. I turned the tap on only to hear the loudest howl, which must have echoed throughout the whole hotel. Slowly, a little water began to drip out. I waited and waited, but the water would not turn warm. I checked the colors on the taps to see that I had turned on the right one. I waited a few more minutes, and to my frustration, it was still cold. As a last resort, I turned off the red one and turned on the blue tap. Within seconds, warm water trickled out! It wasn't much, but it was better than nothing.

I came out of the shower and realized how hungry I was. My father had instructed me to eat only once a day, since we didn't know how long I was going to be stuck in Istanbul and I needed to save my money. The last time I'd had a real meal was in Iran. Now I was starving. But I didn't want to waste time eating. I had important things to do.

I decided I had to dress to impress. I inspected all my clothes, finally settling on a red checkered shirt and beige trousers. I cleaned my black shoes as well as I could. Then I made sure that I had my money and my passport in my pockets. I did not trust the people in the hotel.

It was silent downstairs. Murat was asleep behind his desk, his head in his hands as he snored in pathetic little bursts, while dribbling onto the papers that were scattered on the desk.

I decided against waking him. There were a few old sofas next to the phone cubicles. I sat there, looking for other Iranians and taking in my surroundings: the few plants, the badly painted, stained walls, the holes in the worn carpet. The one thing the lobby did have going for it was the clean window that looked out on the street. I felt safer here in the lobby than I had in my room.

After about twenty minutes, I began to feel bored. As my boredom grew, and the minutes continued to pass, I decided it was time to write my first letter to my mother. I sneaked up to the front desk, where Murat was still snoring, and picked up some paper and a pen and started to write.

Hello Maman,

How are you? I am fine. I am going to the British Embassy today. I am going to tell them that I need a better education. I am going to tell them what Baba told me to say.

He told me that I should never lie to them, because they would find out. But do you remember the program that was on TV a few years ago? The one about my great-grandfather giving money to soldiers to fight the English? Well, I am not sure they will like it if I tell them about our family history. Would it be lying if I did not say anything? Until I get a response from you, I will not say anything. I hope I get a visa, because then I can see cousin Mehdi and tell you how great England is. Will you tell my friends that I beat them there?

I wish that you were here with me. Baba says that I should not say so, but I do miss you, Maman. I wish I could have talked to you last night, but now you know that I am fine. I am nearly ten and can take care of myself. After all, as Mamanjoon says, I am a Kazerooni!

The hotel is really nice, and Istanbul is a very pretty city. I will tell you about my visit to the embassy in my next letter. I have to exchange money before I go there. Don't worry, I will look for the best rate. Hopefully, I will speak to you tonight.

Goodbye!

Your son, Abbas

After I'd completed my first masterpiece, I was idle again. But soon, Murat's squashed and sleepy face rose from the dead.

"Morning!" I said cheerfully.

"Don't you know you shouldn't be so jolly this early?" he said.

I did not quite understand, but I smiled anyway. "Do you have an envelope?"

He held one up, and I grabbed it from him. "Do you want stamps, too?"

"Do you have some?" I asked.

"Sure, just leave the envelope with the address on it here, and I will post your letter for you," he mumbled.

"Thank you," I said, writing down my family's address.

"So why are you up so early?"

"I have to go to the British Embassy," I said, feeling a little less confident, "but first I wanted to see if there are any Iranians here who can tell me how to get there."

"You're cleverer than you look," he said with a smile. "I would take you myself as I have to go into the city, but my shift does not finish until around noon. And you should go as early as you can because the lines get long at embassies."

"I know."

"Well, if you hang around here for a while, some of your countrymen and women will surface soon."

"So there are Iranians here?" I asked, getting excited.

"Oh yes," he said. "Plenty." He yawned and put his head back down on his desk, settling in for another nap.

I looked around the lobby, wondering where all of those Iranians were. I was worried about how the day was going to pan out. I'd never been to an embassy before. Would there be someone there to help me communicate? And if so, what would I say? As I was imagining all kinds of scary scenarios, I heard what I thought was Farsi. I turned toward the voices. A young couple—clearly Iranian—were coming down the stairs.

"Why do we have to leave this early?" I heard the woman say.

"Because we'll get the best deals. It's that simple," the man responded, sounding very sure of himself. "If you don't want to come, then don't."

The couple were both in their early thirties. They were good-looking, but something did not seem right about them. The woman had too much makeup on, and the man could have done with a shave. He had a hard face, and I trusted him less than I did the woman. I had misgivings about talking to either of them, but I decided I had no choice. I smiled as they walked past. "Good morning."

They seemed shocked to see me, but I was obviously Iranian, so they felt obliged to respond with a choruslike, "Morning."

The man's greeting sounded forced. The woman, however, had a genuine smile on her face.

"Are you Iranian?" I asked, knowing full well that they were.

"Yes," the woman replied. "Where are you from?"

"Tehran."

"We're from Mashad."

"Oh, I've been there once with my father," I said quite proudly, "but I prefer Tehran." This time they both smiled.

"Are you here on holiday with your parents?" the lady asked.

"No, I'm here alone." My voice was serious, but they both laughed. Did they think I was joking?

"Really, I am here alone. I have come to get a visa for England."

"Really?" the woman asked.

"I got here last night, and I was waiting to see if anyone can tell me where I can change money. I also need to know where the embassy is."

"How much money do you need to change?" the man asked. I was not sure if I should answer him or not.

There was an awkward silence, and then the lady rescued me. "It's all right," she said. "You don't have to say, darling. We can show you where to go to swap money, but I am not sure where the embassy is because we are here on holiday." I could tell that she was concerned.

"If you give me the directions, I can get there," I said. I was still worried about the embassy, but at least this would be a good start.

"Okay," the man said, "you have to go left as soon as you leave the hotel. Then go straight until you hit the main road. It's a busy road with nice buildings. Then turn right toward the big mosque and keep going until you reach a big indoor market. That's where all the jewelers swap money."

"Thank you," I said. "I really appreciate it. Have a lovely day." Then I got out of my chair and headed out.

I was partway out the door when I heard the woman start to shout at the man. It was obvious that they were arguing about me. I kept on walking, thinking that with a bit of luck, they might offer to show me the way to the market themselves.

Sure enough, the next thing I heard was, "Hey, Kid." It was the man, with the woman in hot pursuit. I waited on the pavement, trying hard not to show my glee, pretending I was surprised that they had followed me.

"Sweetie," the lady said, catching her breath, "you know what? We are going in that direction, and we can show you where it is."

"Thank you," I said politely. The man still seemed to have some reservations about me. He barely spoke.

"What is your name?" the lady asked as we started on our way.

"Oh, sorry; I am Abbas," I said.

"I'm Assal, and this is my husband, Ali."

"Nice to meet you," I said to both of them. I stopped walking and offered my hand for a formal handshake.

When we hit the main road, taxis, cars, and vans were all jockeying for space. Horns were blaring, and sidewalks were crowded with noisy pedestrians. The buildings rose tall and impressive, but it was the mosque in the distance, the one we were heading toward, that impressed me the most. It had a central dome with several smaller domes around it and three or four towers. It was magnificent! It reminded me that Istanbul had once been at the center of a major empire.

I could not believe how busy this part of the city was. Every so often, I would hear a family walking past talking in Farsi. It was true—the place was teeming with Iranians.

Still, I found it difficult to cope with the sheer size of Istanbul and the number of people pushing past me. I knew I could

ABBAS KAZEROONI

easily get lost in this big place, and I was glad that Assal and Ali
were with me. I kept checking my pockets to make sure that
my passport and money were safe. My paranoia eventually led
me to walk with my hands in my pockets, clutching both. I
was happy to let Ali and Assal lead the way.

Eventually, we arrived at a towering entrance to an indoor
market. It was a long, deep market with little stalls and shops
on either side. And just as Ali had promised every third shop
was a jewelry shop.

Ali turned to me. "Well, this is it, Kiddo," he said. "We
usually choose one of these jewelers. It doesn't really matter
which one; they tend to give roughly the same rate."

"Thank you."

Then I saw Assal whisper something in his ear, and he shook
his head, meaning no. "We have to be off," he said abruptly.
"Good luck, and maybe we'll see you later at the hotel."

"Okay," I said. "I'll see you later. Thank you." As they began to walk away, Assal turned and gave me a little wave. I was
trying to remember how we had come, so that I could find my
way back. As I was going over all the streets in my mind, I lost
Assal and Ali in the crowd. I took a deep breath and knew that
my day was about to begin for real.

I turned toward the first jeweler on my left. A bell rang as I
walked into the shop and discovered hundreds of gold items
on display. A man came out from the back of the shop. He
was well dressed; his shirt was not expensive but was nicely

84

ironed. More importantly, he had kind eyes. He smiled at me and asked in Farsi, "How can I help you?"

"You speak Farsi?" I asked.

"Yes, I do," he said.

"How did you know I am Iranian?"

"I can tell," he said with a chuckle. "I see enough Iranians every day to tell the difference."

I smiled back. "Do you exchange dollars for lira?"

The man grinned. "Of course. Today's rate is 980 lira per dollar."

I was pretty sure he was being fair, but I could not take any chances. So I just said, "Thank you, I will be back in a while."

"No problem," he said, "take your time."

I left the shop and ventured through the market. Every merchant was trying to sell his wares to me, and the word no did not seem to exist in their vocabularies. The products varied from backgammon boards to handmade furniture to gold-plated tea sets to cutlery. I was overwhelmed. It was not so easy ignoring everyone or saying no. Shopkeepers would follow you and do absolutely anything in order to make a sale.

Off I went into nearly every jeweler's shop to ask for the dollar rate. Almost without exception, every shopkeeper spoke Farsi, and their rates varied from 950 to 980 lira for a dollar. That very first man had given me the best rate. To be fair, everyone had given me a rate close to that, and no one had tried to cheat me, which made me feel good.

I had to go back to the entrance of the market anyway, so I decided I would swap money with the first dealer, since I liked him the best and trusted him the most, too.

When I opened his shop door, he was waiting.

He smiled in his gentle way. "So I gave the best rate, eh?"

"Equal best," I said. "Two others gave me the same rate."

"They were both at the other end of the market, right?" he asked.

"Yes," I said, surprised. "How do you know?"

"It's my job!" he said with a smile. "But you did come back to me, and for that I want to give you an even better rate, Little Man." This was the second person who had referred to me as "little man" and, quite honestly, I liked it.

"What rate?"

"How does one thousand lira for a dollar sound to you?" he asked.

"I'll take it." I got the fifty-dollar bill out of my pocket and placed it on the counter. My hand was still on the bill, and as his hand reached for it, I did not let go. He smiled once again, opened his till, counted out the lira in front of me, and placed the money next to my hand. Slowly I took my hand off the fifty to gather up the pile of Turkish money. I wanted to count the lira, but I thought I should wait until I had left the shop.

He said, "You come to me again, and I guarantee the best rate. What do you say?"

I shrugged, trying to look casual. "Okay."

I was feeling proud of myself. Not only had I managed to get the best dollar rate in Istanbul that day, but I had also made a good contact for the future. I could not wait to tell my father.

"My name is Hector. If you need help with anything, I'm your man."

"Thank you, Hector," I said politely. "My name is Abbas." I started to leave when I remembered what I still had to do. "Hector?"

"Yes?"

"I want to go to the British Embassy," I said. "I don't suppose you know where it is and if there is a bus that goes that way?"

Hector smiled at me.

"It's your lucky day, Little Man," he said, "because not only do I know where it is, but I know which bus you need, too." He came out from behind his counter and walked to the door as if to point something out. Then he said, "You know what? It is much easier if I just show you."

He pulled out a set of keys, locked the door behind him, and shouted something in Turkish to another stallholder. To me he said, "The bus stop is only a two-minute walk from here."

We walked through the crowded streets and did not really talk; the commotion around us made it difficult. Minutes later, we arrived at a bus stop. I thought Hector would leave, but instead, he took out a pack of cigarettes and offered me one.

"No, thanks, I don't smoke."

He smiled. "A good thing. They are very bad for you." He took one out and lit it, inhaling hard before continuing. "The bus stops right outside the embassy." He puffed out. "I will tell the driver to drop you there. When you're done, wait at the bus stop across the road from where you get off."

"It's that simple?"

"That simple," he said. I liked talking to Hector. He treated me like a friend, not a child.

Buses came and went, and then, with a start, Hector threw his cigarette on the ground. "Here it is." He was waving frantically and shouting like a maniac. As the bus came to a screeching halt, Hector looked at me again. "Do you have a hundred-lira note?"

"Yes."

"Give it to me." The bus stopped and Hector jumped ahead of me and began to talk to the driver in Turkish. He then put the note into a ticket machine—not a ticket as I had expected.

"I told him to drop you outside the embassy," he shouted above the noise of the engine. "You don't need a ticket when you come back; just put another hundred-lira note in the machine and it will be fine." Then he jumped off the bus.

"Thank you very much," I said, amazed that he was doing all this for me.

"Don't mention it." He smiled back. "Just remember me when you change money."

"I will," I said, waving goodbye. I made my way to the back of the bus and sat quietly next to a window.

I did try to look out of the window, but I cannot remember anything I saw. My heart was beating at three times its normal pace. I was trying to foresee all the possibilities that could arise at the embassy. What if there were no Iranians there? What would I do then? At no point did I think about not going. I knew that I just had to give it a shot.

Suddenly, the bus stopped and the driver gave a shout, waving at me to get off.

It turned out that the embassy was actually a consulate. The famous Union Jack flew proudly at the tower. Huge black towering gates stood in front of the building, and two armed guards stood motionless as I approached.

I checked my pockets for my passport one more time. Slowly, I approached the gates, but to my surprise nothing happened. The gates did not open. I looked at one of the guards. He seemed to be completely ignoring me, so I looked at the other guard. He was looking at me, but he said nothing. "Can you let me in, please?" I asked.

They continued to ignore me. I couldn't believe it. I went up to the gates and began to pull on them as hard as I could. One of the guards came over and removed my hands from the gates. He said something that I did not understand. I said, "I need to go in," this time pointing at the building in the distance. "Please let me in."

Once again, he said something in Turkish. It was clear that he did not intend to let me in. I got my passport out and started to wave it at them. "Please let me in," I screamed. "I am an Iranian citizen, and I want to apply for a visa."

I think my frustration merely amused the two guards. They were laughing at me. I did not know what to do, and without even realizing it, I started to cry. "I am not leaving until you let me in," I sobbed.

I walked up to the gates and sat down, holding tight to the bars as I continued to cry. One of the guards came over and said something that must have been an order for me to move, as he was waving his hands to suggest I go away. I didn't budge. Then the guard lifted me up in one scoop and put me down at the edge of the pavement, away from the gate. Much to the guard's frustration, I immediately rose to my feet and ran back to reclaim my earlier position. He frowned as he picked me up again and put me back on the pavement.

He was beginning to get angry, and his tone was changing, but I was determined to stay. This little standoff was repeated another five times until I was back at the gates again. The guard knew he had to try something else. He went into the gate tower and picked up a phone, all the time watching me.

I was still crying when he came out and said something. Once again, I had no idea what he was talking about, so I just sat there, still holding on to the bars. This time he just waved me gently away and, again, went to speak into the phone. Again, I stood my ground.

The guard looked at the other guard, and they both smiled at me. He came over to me again and lifted me up. I thought our game was back on. But he didn't put me down. Instead, I saw the other guard open the gates, and I was carried through into the consulate grounds. I was not sure what was going on, and so I started to kick the guard holding me. I was scared. Were they going to beat me? As soon as I was through the gates, however, he just put me down, shut the gates, and they took up their usual positions.

I kept checking behind me to see if I was being tricked. I could not help but be overwhelmed by the sheer size and beauty of the consulate. A driveway led me to the main entrance of the building, about four hundred feet away from the gates. On either side of the drive were splendid gardens manicured to the minutest detail. The lawns were mowed to the exact millimeter, the roses were in prime condition, and the trees offered shade to the carefully tended smaller plants. To me, it looked like all the stories that I had heard about the West were true. This place was like a fairyland. I was impressed.

For the first time since I had arrived in Istanbul, I had hope. Maybe what my father was doing was right. Maybe England was the best place for me—if it was going to be just like the consulate.

At the entrance to the main building was a large oak door with huge handles. It was half-open, and I remember wondering if I was doing the right thing by going straight through it. Inside was a small corridor with more guards and a man who seemed like a manager of some kind. They stood by a glass door at the far end.

I was not sure what to do until one of the guards waved at me. I walked slowly toward him, and he patted me down to see if I was carrying anything dangerous. Then the manager pointed to a little machine that had small tickets coming out of it. I pulled one out and then looked at the man to see what I should do next. He gestured, suggesting that I should sit down in the area beyond the glass doors. He pointed to a display with red numbers on it. I realized that it would be my turn when my number was shown.

My first impression was that the consulate was like a large post office, with window after window of clerks attending to people. The waiting area was packed. The number being displayed was seventy-eight, and my ticket said one hundred and fourteen. I knew that I would have to wait a long time.

I was nervous. While the first part of my problem had been dealt with—I had found the consulate and managed to get inside—now I had another problem. I was listening to the conversations at the different counters. They were being conducted in either English or Turkish. I could not understand, either.

I leaned over and put my head in my hands. I tried to blank everything out and think. Numbers were flashing and disappearing, and yet nothing was happening. I wanted my parents to be with me so badly. How could I do this on my own? My luck was bound to run out soon. But the thought of disappointing my father always kept me going.

Then I heard someone speaking Farsi say, "Is that little boy crying?"

It was the voice of a beautiful Iranian lady. She was very sophisticated looking and seemed kind, gazing at me as if I were her own child. She sat next to a man, probably her husband. I found myself smiling through my tears.

"Are you alone?" she asked me. She was speaking quite loudly, as she was across the room from me. I nodded to tell her that I was. "Would you like me to come and sit with you?" she asked kindly. I nodded again.

It was then that I realized my biggest weakness was also my biggest strength. My age made people notice me. It made them want to help me.

The lady made her way over to me.

"Hello," she said, sitting down next to me.

"Hello," I said quietly, aware of the impression I was making.

"What's wrong, sweetheart?" she asked, sounding concerned.

I looked at her with my teary eyes and said, "I'm here alone to apply for a visa, and I don't speak Turkish or English." She looked shocked as I added, "I don't know what to do."

"You're here alone?" she asked again.

"Yes."

"Where are your parents?" she asked,

"In Tehran. They wouldn't let my mother out of the country, and my father didn't want me to go to war," I explained, "and now I don't know how to speak to those people." I pointed toward the counters.

The lady was looking even more upset now. She was still trying to get over the shock of my being alone in a foreign country. "Would you like me to help you?" she asked.

"What's your number?"

"Oh," she said as she checked her ticket in her hand, "one hundred and three."

"Mine will come up much later than yours," I said, showing her my number. "You'd have to wait an hour or so."

"It's okay," she said gently as she rubbed my back. "I'll wait with you and translate."

"Oh no, you don't have to do that," I said. Of course I hoped that she would do exactly that, but I was practicing the great Persian tradition of *tarof*. There is no direct translation in English, but it roughly means when one insists on not accepting hospitality or a favor just to be polite.

"Don't be silly," she said. "It will be my pleasure. Just let me tell my husband."

She glided over to her husband and whispered to him. The man looked up and stared at me. It seemed that he wanted no part of this. I didn't blame him. In those days, everyone had their own problems, and the unwritten rule was that you went about your business and did not involve yourself in other people's problems. Everyone was short of money, and all that Iranians in Istanbul cared about was getting to the West. No one wanted to ruin his own chances by becoming entangled in someone else's business unnecessarily.

Eventually, their number was called. When they came back from the counter, a good twenty minutes later, the man walked straight out. I thought that the lady had changed her mind, too, and my heart sank. Now I really was in a jam. There were no other Iranians there, and I had very little time. The flashing number was only two or three away from mine.

Suddenly there was a tap on my shoulder. I looked up to see the lady.

"What's wrong?" she said.

"I thought you forgot about me," I said.

"How could I forget such a handsome face?" she said with a smile. "My husband has some business to take care of, but I'll stay for your interview."

"Thank you so much," I said, blushing a little. "It means a lot."

We sat in silence as we waited for 114 to flash on the screen.

It finally appeared and I stood up, feeling relieved. We walked up to the counter together where a man in his midforties sat behind the glass screen. He was bald and had sharp features. A pair of round spectacles covered his small, suspicious eyes. The lady explained that she was translating for me because I spoke neither Turkish nor English. The man looked straight at me without any expression. Even though the lady spoke for me, he kept looking at me throughout the interview.

"Why are your parents not here?" was his first question.

"Because they would not let them leave the country," I explained.

"The government, you mean?" the lady asked to make sure.

"Yes."

The man asked, "So why did your parents send you here alone?"

"Because my father did not want me to die in the war and wanted me to have a good education. My cousin Mehdi is in England, and he has agreed to be my guardian once I am there."

He took my passport and inspected it. He then started talking quickly in English. "Listen to me," he said in an authoritative manner (as the lady translated), "this had better be the truth, or you will never set foot on English soil. Do not ever lie to us. This is a unique case, and we need to see the relevant paperwork. You have to come back with your parents' permission for you to go to England. You have to have your cousin's name, address, telephone number, occupation, status of residency, and his written permission that he is willing to be your guardian."

The lady kindly wrote down all the man's requests on a piece of paper and handed it to me. The man added, "One more thing. Why in the world are you trying to escape from the war in Iran at such a young age?"

Immediately, I said, "Because in Iran the recruitment age

has been lowered, and boys cannot leave the country after they reach nine. Children like me would be picked first."

"Why? Why are you so different?"

"Because my father had links with the Shah and is thought to be anti-establishment."

The man looked at me, then nodded to confirm that he understood. "Okay," he said, "you can go now, but come back with all the paperwork that I have asked for—and I mean *all*."

I smiled at him and decided to practice my limited English. "Thank you very much," I said. The man suddenly stopped being his serious self and smiled at me. I believe that certain moments decide whether people like you or not. And while I had a feeling that this man didn't like many people, he seemed to be warming to me.

On the way outside, I thanked the lady for what she had done.

"It was my pleasure," she said. "Now don't lose that list. Tell your father when you speak to him next."

"He's going to call me tonight," I said.

When we got to the gates, the guards looked at me again. This time I was smiling, and I waved at them. They waved back. I think I made a few friends that day, even if some were harder to make than others.

The lady turned to me and asked, "Will you be able to get to your hotel?"

"Yes, I'll be fine," I said.

She paused to think. "Listen to me, Abbas. I don't know you, but I think that you are a very special boy. Just take care of yourself and stay out of trouble." With that, she gave me a hug and a kiss on my cheeks and walked away.

I did not even learn her name. While I realized I would probably never see her again, once more a brief acquaintance had made a world of difference to me.

Slowly but happily, I crossed the road and waited for the bus. Sure enough, within minutes it appeared. I waved frantically, imitating Hector from earlier on. I got on and took my seat. All I could think about was speaking to my father that night. I hoped that he would let me talk to my mother.

I had only two other problems left for the day: figuring out my way back to the hotel from the marketplace and finding some good, cheap food.

So far, so good.

Seven

The bus dropped me off at the marketplace. I stood in the middle of the jostling crowd, trying to find my bearings. It was just like it had been that morning: the milling people didn't care about anyone else. It didn't matter to them who they elbowed out of the way, or who they scared; they only cared about getting to their destinations as fast as possible. It was a good introduction to city life.

I decided to retrace my steps from the gates of the market back to the hotel, so I crossed the road and walked to the entrance. I hoped that I would recognize the side road that led to the hotel. I knew it was not too far away, but the city was vast and it was easy to get lost. I'd been so worried about keeping my passport and money safe that morning, I had forgotten all about memorizing my path.

Suddenly, I realized that I had written my to-do list on a sheet of hotel stationery after speaking to Baba the night before. It had the hotel's address and telephone number on it, and it was in my pocket. In the worst-case scenario, I could go into a shop and ask someone to show me how to get there. I felt better already. The people did not seem so bad, and they didn't seem to be pushing past me as much. I hadn't thought to bring that piece of paper with me. I only had it by accident. I'd have to think more clearly in the future.

My eyes fell on a shop that I recognized as my landmark for the left turn into my side street. It was a small kebab shop, and I remembered it because the stench of raw meat coming from it had really hit me when I passed it that morning.

I jogged happily down the side road. Immediately, there was a difference from the main street: it was quieter, dirtier, the people were not well dressed, and the buildings were ugly. In the morning, I had not paid too much attention to my surroundings, as I had been distracted by Assal and Ali. Now, once again, the stench of coal and garbage hit me.

I did not understand how people could live in such a place—until it dawned on me that I was one of those people. I was living here because, like them, I had no choice. In fact, I was delighted to be back at the hotel. It was my safety blanket in this foreign place.

Murat was at reception, showered and changed, but clearly tired and far from happy.

"Hello, Murat," I said. "I thought you finished at noon."

"I was supposed to," he told me, "but once again my replacement hasn't arrived. One thing you'll discover is that I'm like the furniture. Always here."

"I see." I chuckled aloud. "But aren't you tired?"

"You get used to it," he said as he took a drag of a cigarette. "Did you have a good day?"

"Yes, thank you."

I purposely kept it short, but curiosity got the better of Murat. "Did you swap money?" he asked.

"Yup," I said, "which reminds me, can I have my dollars back, please? I have the lira for you."

"Oh, sure," he sighed. "Quite the clever one, aren't we, now?"

I laughed, happy that for once I was being accused of being smart! Murat opened the safe and got fifty dollars out of what looked like a pile of American dollars. I gave him my lira, and he counted it to the last bill, surprised that I had handed over exactly the right amount. He gave me back my fifty.

I looked outside. The sun was setting, and I could tell that it was going to be dark soon. "Where can I buy some food and water?" I asked him.

"There's a corner shop about four hundred feet to the right down the street. You can't miss it. It's cheap, but the food is good."

I thanked him and walked out. I was really hungry and thirsty, and my head was pounding. The street looked ominous in the darkening evening, and the distance to the shop seemed like the longest four hundred feet in the world. If anything were to happen, there was nowhere to run. I kept my hands in my pockets, making sure my passport and money were there, and walked quickly.

Finally, I caught sight of a little shop at the corner of a main road. It looked like a cute shop—the only building that was lit and welcoming around my street, besides the hotel. I could smell all its delicacies from afar: the freshly made bread, the cheeses, the meats, and the vegetables.

As soon as I opened the door, I felt like a little boy in a sweet shop. I wanted to buy everything, but I knew that I had to watch what I spent. A kind-looking gentleman was behind the counter, attending to his shelves. There was a toasting machine that smelled so good I felt faint. It was a machine where you would put in a sandwich and push down the top. It would heat the contents of the sandwich—roasted, diced lamb with tomatoes, onions, mushrooms, peppers, and herbs—and toast the bread. I had never seen a toaster like this before. I did not know how to speak Turkish, so I made a noise, "Emm . . ." and then pointed to the meat.

"Iranian?"

"Yes," I said, surprised at his Farsi. "How much is that?"

"This meat," he said with a laugh, "is called *kavurma*—a thousand lira for one sandwich."

"I see," I said. I was always thinking in dollars, and that seemed expensive. "What about the yogurt?"

"Oh that—150 lira for a tub."

I wanted the kavurma, but that price for yogurt sounded much better to me. The yogurt would last me two days. I needed water, too, as I'd been told not to drink the tap water in Turkey. I picked up a small loaf of bread and a tub of yogurt.

"That's all?"

"Thank you, yes," I said politely.

"Are you here on holiday?"

"Yes," I replied briefly as I paid him. I just wanted to get home and eat.

"How long?"

"Not sure."

"Oh, I see," he said knowingly. It seemed like all the Turks were aware of what I was doing there. "So what is your name, Little Man?"

I could not understand it. None of the people who had talked to me knew each other, but everyone kept calling me Little Man. Was it some kind of conspiracy? It made me jumpy, and I wanted to get out of the shop as soon as I could, even though my instincts told me that this was a good man.

Still, I knew I would be visiting his shop again, so I said, "My name is Abbas, *Efendy.*" I had heard others call older men *efendy*, which meant "sir" or "mister."

The man laughed. "I think I will like you, Abbas, but I think I will call you Little Man."

I ran, my fears chasing me like large, looming shadows all the four hundred feet to the hotel. It just wasn't fair. Everything was far too hard. I kept trying to tell myself that it would be all right, and that my father would be pleased with how much I had accomplished that day. I knew that I had done well, and I decided then and there to reward myself every Friday—the resting day in Iran—with a kavurma sandwich. It would be something to look forward to during the week.

At the hotel, I walked past a dozing Murat. I was scared that my things would not be there when I reached my room. However, I found that the bed had been made up with more damp sheets and the bathroom looked a little cleaner. I slid open the cupboards and checked through my clothes, my papers, my family photographs. Everything was intact.

I stopped at the pictures, especially those of my mother. I missed her unbearably. I could not forget the way she had looked at the airport—on her knees, sobbing. I felt guilty for obeying my father. It was as if I had betrayed a sacred bond between my mother and myself. I had let her down by not even hugging her or kissing her goodbye.

I lay the pictures down on the bed so that I could look at them while I ate. I could just imagine Mamanjoon asking me if I wanted tea. I gulped down a third of the water in one shot, neatly broke the loaf of bread in half, and dipped a piece in the yogurt.

How good that tasted! I thought about how, only a month ago, I would have wrinkled up my nose at such a measly offering. A month before, my biggest concern had been persuading Mamanjoon to give me a snack.

Things had certainly changed. Here I was living by myself, taking care of everything on my own. This was my first meal alone, and as before, the first was the hardest. I missed my mother's cooking and our conversations at meal times. I missed school. But most of all, I missed the security of my home.

When I had eaten half of the yogurt and bread, I put the top back on the pot and placed it by the window to keep it cool. Then I wrapped the bread up in its plastic bag and kept it on the bedside table. I took another few sips of water and placed the bottle next to the bread.

Now what was I to do? It was not even seven thirty and I was bored. I trotted downstairs.

Murat was at his usual post in the lobby.

"Hi," I muttered. "You need to sleep."

"Thanks, Doctor, I'll remember that." He gave me a little smile. I chuckled. I think he got a kick out of trying to entertain me. "There's a television room if you have nothing to do."

"There is?"

"Yeah." He smiled. "Go down the corridor and turn left."

"Great," I said hesitantly, "but I'm waiting for a phone call."

"I'll get you."

"Okay. Thanks, Murat."

This was the first thing that sounded like fun since I had arrived in Istanbul. In Iran there were only two TV channels, and they were mainly programed with shows where famous religious figures would preach Islam.

The corridor led to a small bar at the back of the hotel, which in turn led to the television lounge to its left. It was a small but nice room. There were a few Iranians sitting there drinking tea or beer.

I settled down at the back of the room to watch whatever the other guests were watching. It was called *Knight Rider*. What a show! It blew my mind. The hero and his sporty talking car would save the world against all odds and take out the baddies along the way. I loved it! All the Iranians were talking about it and how famous it was in the West. I could roughly make out what was going on. It was the car that excited me. It was amazing how it could see, talk, and help the hero in defeating evil in the world.

I sat there for a few hours. The programs were amazing. I had never seen an advertisement before, either. I loved them, too. I forgot about everything else. Suddenly, there was a little tap on my shoulder.

"Hello, you." It was Assal. I was quite happy to see her, as everyone in the lounge had company except me. No one had said anything to me, and I had kept to myself.

"Hello, Assal. Nice to see you again."

"You're such a sweet little boy," she said gently, patting my cheek, which made me blush a little. "Your mother taught you good manners."

"Yes, she did," I said quietly.

"So how did it go today, sweetheart?"

"Oh, good, thanks," I said excitedly. "I swapped fifty dollars for a really good rate and then went to the consulate." I was excited that I had achieved all this, and in my excitement, I gave away a little more information than I should have. "They told me about all the papers I need to get. My father is calling tonight, so I'll tell him what to send me."

"You are a clever boy, aren't you?"

I took that as a compliment and grinned back proudly.

"So what was your really good rate, then?" a deep voice asked. Ali had crept up from behind and heard some of our conversation. I didn't want to say anything, but I was cornered. I thought that I should tell the truth, so I could find out if I had been swindled.

"A thousand lira a dollar."

"A thousand?" Assal squealed.

"No way," Ali said with an arrogant smile. "He's lying." He walked off, not even bothering to listen to what I had to say.

"I didn't lie, Assal," I said angrily. "I don't lie."

"I believe you, sweetheart."

"Why doesn't he like me?" I asked. "What have I done to offend him?"

"Nothing, my darling," she muttered, looking embarrassed. "He doesn't like anyone."

"Surely he likes you," I said. She looked at me in a way that suggested the opposite, but smiled through her sadness.

"Yes, sweetheart." She was not fooling anyone. It was obvious that she was unhappy. "Do you want a glass of tea?"

"Oh, no, thank you," I said. My budget was very important to me, and I knew I could not afford such luxuries.

"It's okay, sweetheart. I'll buy it for you."

"You don't have to do that," I said. "I have money."

"I know you do, but I want to treat you."

I didn't want her to buy tea for me, and I didn't want to buy it for myself either, so I declined her offer one more time.

"I insist," she said stubbornly.

I watched her go to the bar and order the tea. On her way, she said hello to a few Iranians, dropping her voice low. I pretended not to be listening, but I could hear some of what she was saying. She was telling them that I was alone, and what a nice boy I was. I could hear all the "ahs" and "bless hims." I pretended to watch television, but I could see out of the corner of my eye that, one by one, everyone was turning to have a look at me. I could sense that the women were drawn to me, while the men were not as interested.

About ten minutes later, Assal came back with the tea. She put it down in front of me. "Enjoy, Abbas," she said. She had tears in her eyes. Her tone of voice was so sad and low that only I could hear what she was saying. "You take real good care of yourself, you hear me?"

"Yes, I will," I said, surprised. She was making me nervous. Why was she speaking to me like that?

"Istanbul can be a nasty place."

Then she kissed me on the cheek and left. Honestly, I could have done without her last comment. I was scared enough. Now I was frightened for her, too. Something was not right.

• • •

I had completely forgotten about my father's phone call. Around ten thirty Murat ran into the lounge and called out, "Abbas, quick!" I jumped to my feet and ran toward the cubicles, reaching inside my pocket for the list of documents I needed to get. Murat held up his index finger to indicate the first cubicle.

"Maman?" I shouted hopefully.

"No, it's me," my father said.

"Oh, hi, Baba. Can I speak to Maman?"

"No, Abs, she's ill at the moment. Maybe tomorrow, if she's feeling better." I could tell he was lying.

"Okay," I said, trying to hide my disappointment. There was a pause as my father gathered his thoughts. I didn't speak. I wanted to talk to my mother, and he was not letting me.

"How are you?" he asked.

"Good, thanks," I said. "And you?"

"Oh, we're all fine, apart from your mother, who has the flu or something."

"Tell her I said hi."

"I will," he replied. "So what happened today?"

"Sorry?" I was still in my own little world, thinking about my mother.

"The embassy and the money-changing," he snapped. "Come on, Abs. Get on with it."

I could not believe he was shouting at me. Tears were rolling down my cheeks, but I was determined not to let him know.

"Sorry, Baba," I said. "I went to the market this morning and checked with all the money dealers, and I got the best price in town."

"Which was?"

"A thousand lira to a dollar."

"Don't lie to me, Abs," he said.

"I got a thousand. Why does everyone think I am lying? I never lie."

"All right, Abs." He paused. "Did you really get that much?"

"Yes," I snapped. "I swapped only fifty dollars because the rate changes every day, like you said."

"Good boy," he said. "That is amazing! I don't think I could have done any better myself."

"Probably not. Nobody did today." There was a silence. He must have noticed the arrogance in my tone, but I honestly didn't care. I felt unappreciated and unloved.

He decided to ignore it. "And the embassy?"

"I went there by bus, and I spoke to a man. He told me that I need your written permission for me to go to England, Mehdi's full name, address, telephone number, occupation, status of residency, and his written permission that he is willing to be my guardian."

"He told you all that?"

"Yeah."

"And you remembered it all?"

"Yes, but I also wrote it down."

"I see," he said, sounding surprised. "You did this all by yourself?"

"No. I can't speak English or Turkish, so I asked an Iranian lady for help. She agreed to translate."

There was a long pause. I guessed he could not understand how I had accomplished all this.

"Well done."

I decided not to thank him. After all that, all I got was a "well done"?

"So how are you?" he went on.

"Good," I said. "The hotel is great. The area is really nice in the day and . . ."

"You're not spending too much, are you?"

I felt sad and annoyed at the same time. I was going out of my way to make him proud, but did he have any faith in me? Did he understand what I was going through, and how difficult it was? I was depressed, I was scared, I was hungry, I was paranoid, and he did not seem to understand any of this.

"No, Baba, I only bought my bus tickets, paid for my hotel, got my dollars back, and to eat, all I bought was a loaf of bread, a pot of yogurt, and a bottle of water."

"That's it?"

"I swear."

"Okay." He paused again. "You're a good lad. Just stay in the hotel. Don't leave unless you have to, and certainly don't go out at night. I will send you the documents as soon as I can. I will call you the day after tomorrow, at night. I can't call every day, Abs. It's very expensive. The papers will be with you soon—in about seven to ten days, I should think."

"That long?"

Yet another pause. Tension filled the line. "I know, Abs. You're just going to have to be strong for me, all right?"

"I will."

"You take care."

The phone clicked. I couldn't believe it. I had thought my father would be proud of me—and that he would say it. I wished he had not called at all. I knew it must be hard for him, and for my mother too, but at least they had each other.

EIGHT

I returned to the television lounge and slid into the back row of seats to hide my misery in the darkness. My mind was still on the conversation with my father, and suddenly watching television was no longer appealing. Would my father ever be the same with me again, now that I was here in Istanbul? He had always set high standards for me, and they were always a challenge. However, this was too hard.

I stayed in the lounge until about two in the morning Everyone else had gone to bed. The hardest thing for me so far had been falling asleep in that hotel room, where every noise and every shadow seemed like a potential threat. I noticed a smiling Murat at the door.

"Not tired?"

"No," I lied.

"You like this?" He pointed to the television. It was playing a documentary on truck drivers in Turkey. I shrugged to say that I did not mind.

"I'm practicing to be a receptionist like you," I said with a straight face. I could tell Murat was trying not to smile as he left.

Finally, I switched off the television and wandered to reception. Murat stood by the lobby door, smoking a cigarette. "Going to bed?"

"Yup," I said. "I thought I would come and say goodnight first." It was yet another excuse to put off going upstairs.

"Oh," he said with surprise. "Thank you."

There was a pause as I desperately tried to think of something to say. "Are you on all night?"

"Well, until five a.m. supposedly," he sighed, "but we'll see if that actually happens or not." I did not have anything else to say. I was about to turn away when he said, "What are your plans for tomorrow?"

"Nothing."

"You have no business to take care of?" he inquired.

"No, I'm waiting for some paperwork, so . . ."

"I know." He smiled. "You have to kill time without spending money." I nodded. He obviously knew what was going on. "It's okay," he said. "We have things to do to kill time here."

"Does it cost anything?" I asked.

"Free!"

"Well, what is it?"

"For that, my friend, you have to wait until tomorrow."

"Goodnight, Murat," I said with a smile. I liked him more

and more, because even in his casual way he seemed to care about me.

"Goodnight, Abbas."

I was about to walk off when my curiosity got the better of me. "Murat?"

"Yes?"

"Have any children my age stayed here before?" I asked and then completed the question. "Alone, I mean."

Murat looked at me knowingly. "No."

"Okay," I said softly, "thank you." It made me feel special—and, of course, proud—because I was the first. On the flip side, it made me feel scared, because I did not know if I was capable of getting through what was ahead.

I headed upstairs and through the dark corridor to my room. My mother had always told me that doing something for the first time was the hardest. I was waiting for this part to get easier, but it seemed as difficult as the first night.

Slowly, I opened the door and peeped inside the room. Everything was as I had left it. The smell of dampness and the breeze squeezing through the gaps in the window immediately hit me. One would think that a hotel room would have been a place of solace, but it was far from that.

I entered and locked the door behind me. I could hear all kinds of little noises: the cockroaches, the wind, and every person who wandered past on the street. I swiftly drew the curtains so that no one could see me. Then I got my photographs out and placed them on the second pillow on the bed. I walked into the bathroom to brush my teeth. The cockroaches were dancing in the corners as usual. I brushed and brushed. It brought a little smile to my face, thinking how, back home, I would do everything I could to avoid this nightly routine.

I pulled back the sheets to get in. For the second night running, I could not bring myself to turn the lights off. The sheets were dank again, and I hated the thought of trying to sleep on them. I could not look at the picture of my father that night. I held my mother's photograph, and then I looked up as if to God. Mamanjoon always prayed; in fact, she prayed so often that she must have prayed on our behalf, too! However, neither of my parents prayed regularly. I wasn't sure I knew how.

But I whispered, "God, I don't know why this is happening to me. If I have done anything wrong, I'm really sorry. If I have to be punished and cannot return home, then so be it, but please let Maman come soon. I'm not sure how long I can do this. If I must be punished alone, then please help me get through it."

The day had taken its toll on me, and my thoughts were helter-skelter. How long was I going to have to wait? Was my father angry with me, or disappointed? When would I be able to see my mother again, or at least speak to her? What was I going to do while waiting for my papers? I must have started crying, because the light shattered into starlike fragments as I stared at it until somehow I fell asleep.

• • •

The next morning I woke up very early again. It was not quite day yet so I lay back, jumping in and out of dreams. Finally, I rose grudgingly from my bed. My skin was red and raw from the cold. I dared not say anything to Murat. I was too scared to ask for anything—even a blanket. What would happen if I had to swap hotels? My father was sending the documents, and I might not receive them. In addition, I didn't know if I could face the trauma of having to find another hotel. I might not be lucky enough to find another taxi driver as kind as Ahmed.

I bathed and put on some clothes, though I had nowhere to go. I kept my money and passport in my pockets. I was about to open the door when I saw the bread. It was very tempting, but I decided to have my meal at the end of the day to reward myself for getting through it. I walked out.

The first thought of every day was what to do with my money, the second was whether I should eat then or later, and the third was to wonder if my father was still angry with me. *Maybe tonight will be easier,* I thought as I locked the door and went downstairs.

I was expecting a new receptionist, but Murat was there.

"I thought you were . . ."

"So did I," he said with a sigh. "So did I."

"Do you ever sleep?"

"It appears not." He yawned. "The—" He proceeded to

call the absent replacement a name, then instantly covered his mouth with his hand. "I'm sorry."

"It's okay," I said, laughing. "I know all the bad words."

He chuckled. "Well, this is the fourth time this new guy has let me down, but when you have your own business, you have to make sacrifices."

"That's what my father says."

"He's a wise man," he said.

"Is this hotel yours?" I asked.

"Half mine."

"Whose is the other half?"

"You ask a lot of questions, Little Man," he said with a smile.

"So do you," I retorted without thinking.

"Yes, you're right," he said, "that I do." He sat up in his chair and lit a cigarette. "The other half of the hotel belongs to a silent partner." He saw that I was looking at him blankly. "That means he does not work here. I make all the decisions."

"So you are the boss?"

"I am!"

"Cool."

Murat chuckled again as he puffed on his cigarette. "Not so cool when you don't sleep," he said. "What are you going to do with yourself today?"

"I'm not sure, really . . ." It was clear that I was out of ideas.

"Why don't you write another letter to your parents?"

"I could do that," I replied. "Oh, by the way, did you . . ."

"Yes, I sent it in the post yesterday. If you want any more paper and a pen, just help yourself." He handed me some paper, a pen, and a few envelopes.

"Thank you, Murat," I said softly. "How much do I owe you for the stamp yesterday?"

"Oh, nothing," he said with a wave of a hand. "Just don't tell anyone else, that's all. This is a deal only for my favorite customers."

I smiled and touched my nose. "Our little secret," I said. "Thank you very much."

"Thanks for what?" Murat gave me a little wink.

I walked over to the sofa next to the phone booths and decided this letter was definitely not going to be addressed to my father; so I began to write my second letter to my mother.

Dear Maman,

How are you? I am doing very well. As I am sure you know, yesterday I went to the city to exchange money. I went to a very big market with all sorts of dealers. They are really pushy! Anyway, I found a really good man who gave me the best rate in Istanbul. I got a thousand lira for a dollar. Baba thought I was lying, but you know that I don't lie, Maman. The city is really beautiful, with really big buildings everywhere. There is this huge mosque, which you can see from everywhere.

I wish you were here, too.

After exchanging the money, I went to the British Consulate. I caught the bus there! It was fun and it was cheap. Here they just let you put the money in a machine. You don't even need a ticket! I had to wait a long time at the consulate, and I was scared at first, but a really nice lady helped me. The man there asked me to get all these papers. I'm sure Baba has told you what I need. So here I am, waiting to receive them. The television channels are so much better than they are at home. My favorite program is called Knight Rider. *It is so cool! However, I have only seen programs that were on last night. Maybe next time I will have a different favorite!*

You would be proud of me, as I am having at least a shower every day and brushing my teeth twice a day like you taught me. I am also eating only once a day like Baba told me to. I get hungry sometimes, but if I keep myself busy, I forget.

I really hope to speak to you soon, Maman, as I miss you so very much.

Your son, Abbas

P.S. Please don't tell Baba that I was scared at the consulate.

I sealed the letter inside the envelope and addressed it, leaving it for Murat to post. It was mid-morning. I thought the television room was worth a try, but it was being cleaned, so I returned to the lobby to find Murat with yet another tea, looking cross.

"What's wrong?" I asked.

"Have you seen that lady Assal and her husband?"

"Not since last night," I said. "Why?"

"They have left without paying."

"How?" I asked. "You take the money in advance."

"Not from old customers."

"Oh," I said, disappointed that I'd had to pay up front.

"What? Don't look at me like that. If you stay more than four weeks, you can pay at the end of every week because we would have built trust by then."

"I thought we already had."

"Yes, we have," he said, "but, believe me, it's not like that with everyone else."

"I guess not."

"So with them, well, they stayed six weeks, and then they asked for credit. I gave it, because they had paid up before that."

"How did they get away?"

"I think the husband left first and waited on the street and then the woman threw their bags out of the window in the middle of the night," he explained. "I saw her leave at around 2 a.m."

As I listened to Murat, I thought about what Assal said to me the last time I saw her and how kind she had been to me.

"I'm sorry," I said.

"So am I," Murat sighed. "It's not the first time, and it won't be the last. Oh, by the way, don't tell anyone about the credit thing."

"I won't," I said with a smile. I touched my nose again.

"Good," he said. "Then after next week, you can pay at the end of every week. Okay?"

"For real?" I asked.

"Yeah," he said, "but if anyone finds out about this, our deal is off."

"I promise."

He offered his hand and I shook it firmly.

"What are you planning to do with the rest of your day, Little Man?"

I shrugged.

"Okay," he said with a devilish smile. "I know what I can teach you to do."

"What?"

"Patience," he said. "All good things come to those who wait." He returned to his desk and picked up some papers. "Once I've got through these, I'll show you."

He started to work while I sat silently on the sofa and watched him. He was young, but work had aged him, putting large puffy bags under his eyes. I could tell he was a nice man, but he always looked troubled, even when he seemed happy. Something in his eyes told me that. I found myself wishing there was some way I could help him.

A few people came and went through the lobby. Two guys in particular caught my attention. They were young and badly dressed. Their clothes were torn, their hair was messy, and they were obviously high on something. I could see Murat's look of disapproval as he stared at them until they left.

He looked at me and said, "They're not going to be staying here tonight."

I never did see how he evicted them, but that moment was an important one for me. Murat's hotel was by no means the Hilton, but he had standards. It made me feel a little bit easier.

A good hour passed.

"So then, Little Man, do you have any idea what I am about to teach you?" Murat put the papers aside and turned to me.

"No," I said impatiently.

"What we are about to do requires tea," he announced grandly.

"Oh," I said, "do I have to have one?"

"You don't *have* to," he said with a smile, "but if you want to play like a real Turk, then you need to."

"I see." I wanted tea but did not want to spend my money.

"It's okay," Murat smiled. "You're playing with the boss, remember, which makes the tea free. Two glasses of tea coming up." He started to go into the kitchen, then turned quickly to look at me. "By the way," he noted, "this free tea . . ."

"I know. Don't tell anyone." I touched my nose again.

He nodded approvingly. "You're learning fast."

Murat came back with two glasses of tea and some sugar cubes on a tray. He also brought a large board, which I immediately recognized as a backgammon board. I had seen my father play the game with his friends in Iran, but I had never played it myself. I was excited.

"Right then, I'm about to turn you into a real Turk," Murat announced as he sat down and opened the board. I did not say anything, as in Iran they made fun of Turks, and I knew what my father would have said to that remark. However, from what I had experienced so far, Turks were nothing but clever and friendly.

Murat spent the first thirty minutes teaching me the main rules. I picked it all up very quickly, so he decided to teach me the subtle tricks and intricacies of the game, too. I don't think he was expecting to take his pupil that far in just a few hours. We then decided to play a game, and in Istanbul, a typical game was the best of five. In my first competitive game against an experienced player, I lost three games to two. Murat swore that he was playing his very best. After the game, he stood up and shook my hand.

"You're a fast learner, Little Man. We'll make a Turk out of you yet."

I took it as a compliment.

"Right, you can practice here if you want," he said. "I need to catch up on my sleep, but later on tonight we'll play another game."

"Great!" I said.

"I'll see you later then."

"Sure . . . but Murat?"

"Yes?"

"Who's going to look after the reception?"

"No one," he said. "If anyone comes in, tell them we have no room."

"Okay."

I stayed put at reception and set the board up for a game against myself. I played happily for hours without even noticing the time. I was learning how to throw the dice and teaching myself new techniques.

Murat reappeared, looking a little fresher. He had had a shower, but he still looked tired.

"You slept only four hours."

"I know," he said with a smile.

"Is that enough?"

"No, but it's four hours more than yesterday. How about you? What have you done?"

"I have played backgammon with myself."

"What? Ever since I left?"

"Yes," I said, "and I helped myself to tea. I hope that's okay?"

Murat looked at me seriously, before realizing that I was joking. "You're a livewire, Little Man," he said with a chuckle, "that's for sure. Talking of tea, could you get me a glass from the kitchen?"

"Who, me?"

"Yes, you," he said, sitting down on a sofa next to me. "It's all right; you can get one for yourself, too. And when you get back, we'll see how good you really are at this game."

"You're on."

I ran to the kitchen and opened the door. I had never been there before. It was disgusting: a small room with rust, mold, and dust monopolizing all surfaces, including the walls. The glasses looked clean, but I washed two under the tap anyway. The pot was on the stove. I poured the tea and walked out to find Murat sitting on the sofa with the backgammon board in front of him, ready to commence battle. Excitedly, I sat down opposite him and off we went. Once again, it was an intense game, and I could see that Murat was really trying. However, this time *I* beat *him* three games to two.

We played silently, but once we were finished Murat looked up at me and said, "You make a good glass of tea."

This made me laugh, as it was completely unrelated to our game, and I had fetched the tea a long time before. Murat did not comment on my playing, but he did not really need to. I knew that I was good.

It was early evening. We had been playing backgammon for hours. Murat reclaimed his throne at reception, and I went to the television lounge. A few people came in and out. There was a little tap on my shoulder. It was the barman. His Farsi was not that great, but he did manage to say, "One minute, come with me, please?"

"Where?" I asked him.

"Just here." He pointed to the reception area. "Please, Murat explain."

As I entered the lobby, I saw Murat with a guy I had never seen before. He was dressed in a good suit and tie and looked very suave, with a neatly trimmed mustache and jet-black hair brushed back with gel. It was a little too smooth for my liking. He and Murat were laughing together.

"Ah," declared Murat, like the host at a party, "this is the little man I was talking about."

"Hello," said the man in perfect Farsi. "My name is Abdul."

"Hello, I'm Abbas." We shook hands, but I was not sure what this had to do with me.

"I understand you only recently learned to play back-gammon."

"Yes, today, in fact."

"Only today?" He smiled at Murat. "Did you tell him to say that?"

"I swear I didn't," Murat replied with a grin.

"Anyway, Abbas," Abdul said as he undid his tie, "Murat seems to think you could beat me at a game of backgammon."

"I'm not sure about that."

"Would you like a game?" Abdul asked.

"I'm not sure," I said, looking to Murat for support.

"Go on, Little Man," Murat encouraged. "It's only a game. You'll thrash him."

"Okay," I said with a small smile.

Murat and the barman sat on either side of me and watched like hawks. No one spoke.

I beat Abdul three games to none. He did not look impressed. Murat jumped up and hugged me. I, too, was happy I had won, but Murat's reaction seemed a little over the top.

Abdul got to his feet, threw a bundle of banknotes on the table, and left without saying goodbye. Murat picked up the bundle and put it in his pocket.

Suddenly I realized what had just happened. Murat had placed a bet on my game. I was angry that I had been so stupid. It had all seemed strange from the start. It was obvious that I had been taken advantage of. I didn't say anything; I just looked at Murat in disgust and walked back to the television lounge.

I heard him call out, "Hey, Little Man, wait up," but I kept walking. Apart from Ahmed and the jeweler, Murat was the only person I had trusted, and he had let me down.

After a few minutes, Murat came into the lounge with a glass of tea.

"Hi, Little Man," he said.

I kept my eyes glued to the television.

"I brought you a glass of tea," he said in an apologetic voice.

"I don't want tea, thank you."

"It's on the house," he said with a smile.

I could not believe the man's audacity. I turned to him and, without a trace of emotion, said, "I think tonight I have paid for all the tea you've given me and more."

He seemed taken aback by my comment, but he was man enough to say, "Okay, you have a point there."

I continued to look away.

"Listen," he said, trying to reason with me, "I'm sorry. I really am. It was wrong of me to bet on you without telling you."

"Yes, it was," I said. "What would have happened if I had lost? You would have blamed me."

"No, I wouldn't have. To be honest, I expected you to lose," he said. "He gave me good odds."

I turned around to glare at him.

"Well, I didn't expect you to win so comfortably, at least," he admitted. "He popped in to see me, and I told him about you beating me, and he said he would bet that he could beat you." He paused to see if I was listening, which I was. "So I accepted the bet. I didn't tell you, because I didn't want you to be under pressure."

I kept quiet.

"Listen, would it be any better if I gave you ten percent of my winnings?"

Without hesitating, I countered, "Twenty-five."

"What?"

"Twenty-five percent, and I'll forgive you."

"You—what? You'll *forgive* me for twenty-five percent?"

"My father taught me that everything has a price," I said. I was seeing the funny side to this now, and I could see an opportunity to make some money.

"Okay," he said with a chuckle, "how about fifteen?"

"How about twenty? And that's my final offer."

He glared at me and then offered his hand so that we could shake on it. "You drive a hard bargain, Little Man!"

"I know," I said. "How much did you win?"

"Thirty thousand lira."

"Crap!" I said. "Okay, you can take one day off my rent and give me a thousand lira in cash. How is that?"

He was laughing. "That sounds fine," he said smiling. "When did you get the time to work all that out in your head?"

I decided it was time to celebrate with dinner. As I was about to go upstairs, Murat called me back. "Er, Little Man?"

"Yes?"

"Do you want to do this again?"

"What? Gamble?"

"Yes," he said in a soft voice.

"I can't," I explained. "I can't afford to lose money, and my father will not be impressed if he finds out."

"Hmm," he said, trying to think and speak at the same time, "what if I gave you an option where you could not lose any money? I'll put the money on you, and I'll find people to play against you, and if you lose, it's my tough luck."

"What? So if I lose, then I would not have to pay anything?"

"Right."

"What?" I asked. "You would not even be upset with me?"

"No," he said, "I promise."

"And if I win?"

"You get a cut, but not twenty percent, because the risk will be all mine."

"How much, then?" I asked.

"I was thinking . . . something like five percent?"

"Really?" I said, smiling. "Because I was thinking fifteen."

"Ten and that's my *final* offer," he said, imitating me.

"Okay, but what about my father?"

"Ah, your father," he said, stopping to think. "Does your father really have to know? After all, it's not you who is gambling. It's me. You'd just be participating in a game, and every so often, I could give you small presents because I like you."

He had sold the idea to me. I could save a lot of money if I kept winning, and maybe get to eat a little more.

"Deal," I said, offering my hand. Then I pulled it away. "Oh, one more thing."

"What *now?*" he asked.

"Only one thing, I promise," I said, giggling. "Can I have unlimited free tea?"

"What?"

"You said yourself that one can't play this game unless one drinks tea," I explained, "so how am I meant to practice without tea?"

I could see the frustration in his eyes, yet he was smiling at the same time. He sighed and said, "Okay, but only if you don't go over the top, and—"

"I know; don't tell anyone!" I touched my nose in the customary manner. Murat chuckled and touched his nose too, like it was our little code. "Umm, Murat?"

"Yes?"

"Can I have my money, please?"

I don't think he could believe his ears.

I grinned. "Well, you do owe me a thousand in cash, and one night's free stay."

"That I do."

"My mother always told me not to lend or borrow, and if you don't pay me now, in a way I'll be lending you a thousand," I explained with a smile, "and then I'd have to charge you interest!"

Murat knew I was joking, but I think he was surprised at my knowledge of money and business. He did not know about my homeschooling in economics.

"Come on, then," he said. "Come and get your money before you kill me."

I followed him to reception, where he opened the safe, fished out a thousand lira, and handed it to me. It was not all that much money, but I was thrilled. I had made my own money in a foreign country!

As I took the cash, I had an idea. I realized that a thousand was not a lot of money, and I would most likely spend it if I had it on me. I wanted to keep it safe, so I turned to Murat and asked, "Could you keep the money I earn in the safe?"

"Sure," he said, surprised.

"So every time I earn money, we add it to the pile, right?"

"Okay," he said hesitantly. "So you don't want it now?"

"No, I just wanted to see it and make sure it is mine!"

"It's okay, Little Man. It's yours."

I knew that I could not carry my dollars on my person for much longer in case I was robbed, but I had to make sure that it would be safe if I left it somewhere. I decided that this would be a good test to see if Murat would look after my money honestly. I would wait to build up a pile of backgammon money, and then at a random time I would ask for it. If Murat gave it to me without question, then I would trust him with my dollars, too. It was far from a foolproof plan, but it was the best I could come up with at the time.

With a good night's work under my belt, I decided it was time to reward myself with a meal of bread and yogurt.

As I chewed in solitude, all I could think about was my parents. This was my first night in Istanbul they had not promised to call me. I watched television for the rest of the evening, turning around every time someone walked in. It got later and later, but I couldn't help hoping they would call, despite what Baba had said about the cost. My winnings and my agreement with Murat seemed like a distant memory. I just longed to hear my mother's voice. I sat there like a lost puppy until I fell asleep.

"Little Man," a voice murmured. "Little Man." It was Murat, trying to wake me up.

"Have I got a call?" I asked, jumping up.

"No," he said with a sad face. "It's late. I thought you might want to go to bed."

"Oh," I groaned, "what time is it?"

"Around four in the morning."

"Sorry."

"You don't have to be sorry," he said. "You can do what you like. I just thought that you'd prefer to sleep in a bed; that's all."

I stood and walked slowly up the stairs. Deep down, I had really thought that Baba would call. I slipped into the damp bed with the lights on and tried to sleep while looking at my family's pictures.

It wasn't getting any easier.

NINE

The next morning I woke up later than usual. I knew that I had a trip to the shop to look forward to that day; I had a letter to write, and of course, I had to eat. For the first time, I could not bank on my father calling me. So I decided to concentrate on the things that were certainties.

I strolled downstairs in my same ripped jeans and took the usual route to Murat's throne. To my great surprise, in his place sat a much younger man who was thin, short, and dressed in his best suit, obviously trying to impress anyone who came into the hotel. His hair was wet and brushed back. He had dark, Turkish features and an irritating, ever-present, pretentious smile.

He stood up from his chair and offered his hand. "You Abbas, yes?"

He kept shaking my hand, as if he had forgotten that he was holding it.

"Yes, I'm Abbas."

"Very nice to meet you. I am Hussein."

"Hello, Hussein," I said, pulling my hand out of his. He was making me a little uncomfortable.

"Boss said I should give you tea and a backgammon board."

"You mean Murat?"

"Yes," he said, his smile stretching even wider. He reached under the reception counter and pulled out the backgammon board. "Please take seat, and I bring you tea." He pointed to my sofa.

"Okay," I said, "but I want to write a letter first, to my mother."

"Idiot Hussein," he said, slapping his head. "I forgot." He immediately pulled out a stamped airmail envelope and two sheets of paper. He handed them to me, still smiling annoyingly. "Just put it back here when you're done. Then we can start playing backgammon."

I looked at him with a faint smile and retreated to my usual sofa next to the phone booths. I couldn't help but stare at the telephones. I could not remember having spent a single day without seeing or talking to at least one of my parents before now.

I picked up the pen and began to write.

Dear Maman,

I hope you and Baba are well. I am really missing you both, especially you, because I have not spoken to you for a long time now. But I am behaving myself! To be honest, I am staying up quite late, but last night it was because I was waiting

*to see if you or Baba would call. You didn't. I think you must
have been busy. I have learned how to play backgammon, and
I think I am quite good, too! I don't have a lot to say today,
because I stayed in the hotel all day yesterday. Maybe I will
have more to tell you tomorrow.*

Your son, Abbas

As I put the letter on the reception counter, the ever-eager
Hussein jumped up with the backgammon board. "How about
a game now?"

I was not really in the mood, but I felt I had to do it, so I
nodded.

"Good," he said, sounding too enthusiastic. "I'll set it up."

"It's okay," I said as I took the board from him. "I know
how." I did not want to play this guy, but I would. I beat him
three games to none, even though my mind wasn't on the
game. I couldn't help thinking about the next few days. What
was I going to do with myself?

Little did I know that my daily routine was going to change
drastically.

After the game, I went back to the lounge, reclined in my
back-row seat, and watched bad daytime Turkish television. I
drifted off to sleep, and in what had become a custom, Murat
woke me with a gentle tap on the shoulder.

"We have work to do, Little Man."

I snapped out of my snooze. "What?"

"I have a few friends who wish to challenge you," he whispered with his mysterious smile.

"When?"

"When better than the present?"

"Now?"

"Aha," he said with a purposeful nod. "Go and wash your face in the kitchen and meet me in the lounge."

He turned and walked off with a bit of a swagger. It scared me a little, as he seemed very confident. I hoped that he had not bet heavily on me. Even though I didn't plan to lose, I suddenly felt I was carrying a large burden. What if I did lose?

As I approached the kitchen, I could hear a lot of noise in the lobby. It sounded like a crowd at a soccer stadium. I went in to find Hussein making twelve teas.

"Hello, my friend," he said, smiling from ear to ear.

"Hi," I said in a daze. "What is going on?"

"You have spectators today."

"What?"

"There is big crowd in reception waiting for the little champion."

"Oh, no," I said, trembling, "this was not in the deal."

"Deal?"

"Nothing," I said quickly. I was nervous. Not only would I be playing against a stranger, but in front of a crowd. Hussein left the kitchen and I dithered, breathless. There was no way I could back out of this now. I turned the tap on and splashed my face with the ice-cold water.

Slowly, I made my way toward the loud voices. I peered around the corner to see what was waiting for me. There was a huge man sitting on one side of the board plus another ten or twelve people all waving money in the air like hooligans. In the midst of this crowd was Murat orchestrating the event.

The man waiting to play must have weighed at least 250 pounds. He had sharp, beady eyes, a receding hairline, a huge bristling shoe brush of a mustache, and a nose that had been broken at least three times. He did not seem the kind of character one would like to encounter in a dark alley late at night. He sat expressionless as he practiced throwing the little dice with his ugly, flabby hands.

I was terrified about playing him. Before entering the reception area, I decided that I would not look at him. I would only look at the board.

As soon as the crowd caught sight of me, they bellowed. The men were shouting and clapping as if I were an international superstar. Deep inside, I liked all the attention, but I was also aware that if I did not live up to the hype, I would soon be ridiculed.

Murat walked over to me and whispered into my ear, "They love you, Little Man." I looked up at him as if I did not care.

"Are you okay?" he asked.

I merely nodded.

The man opposite stared coldly at me, like a wild animal. But I stuck to my plan and did not look at him again, except out of the corner of my eye. As soon as Murat had confirmed

I was ready, there was one more raucous round of shrill shouting and money exchanging hands. Murat yelled out in Turkish. Everyone stopped talking, and the noise simmered down into silence. It was time for me to take center stage.

I picked up a die and threw it. My opponent cast a higher number, and so he started the game. I did not know how much was at stake, but going by the commotion, I gathered that it was a lot. During the first game, I was not relaxed, and it must have been obvious. I did not make a complete fool of myself, but I did make mistakes. My opponent took the first game from me.

I looked up at Murat, who did seem relaxed. He smiled at me and nodded to indicate that all would be fine.

His reassurance gave me confidence. The second game was a hard-fought one, and I won by a small margin. The crowd exploded into cheers again. It was clear the odds were against me, which had seduced the bystanders to bet on me. Now they knew they had a chance.

It suddenly occurred to me: if all these people were betting on me, then who was betting against me, so that Murat could win our money? I realized with a heavy sadness that it must be Murat himself who was betting against me. He must expect that I would lose! And with that, I no longer cared about winning or losing. Once again, Murat had kept me in the dark. I looked up at my opponent. He did not seem so frightening anymore. I smiled at him and then glared at

Murat, who must have then realized that I had figured out his scheme.

I wanted to teach Murat a lesson.

I won the third game, too.

The fourth game was close, but my opponent took it. Now we were even. Everything depended on the fifth game.

The man was sweating heavily. Murat was looking edgy, and so was the crowd. It struck me that I could win, then play dumb, and claim money from Murat anyway. My only mistake had been that I had not asked him how much money he had bet on me. Either way, though—win or lose—I was determined to get cash out of this. I was in a win-win situation, and I was beginning to enjoy myself. Once again, Murat had underestimated me.

The final game was a cinch. I had luck with the die and I played well. It was the quickest game, and when I won, the crowd went crazy. They screamed and clapped, and one by one, they came up to me and kissed me and then lifted me on their shoulders. Someone even tried to give me a beer!

I looked at Murat out of the corner of my eye. He was sitting behind the reception desk, counting money out of the safe. He was upset, but when his eyes met mine he tried to hide it. I think he knew that I knew, but he was not going to say anything.

There was a tap on my shoulder. My massive opponent was towering over me, and he smiled as we shook hands.

Then I turned to go, because I did not want to be near them when they started to exchange money. It made me uncomfortable.

I walked to the lounge, only to be greeted by a horde of Iranian guests cheering heartily. I sat down, blushing and not knowing where to look.

One of the men yelled out, "Hey, kid, what's your name?"

"Abbas."

"Mr. Abbas," he said, "that was some game."

"Thank you," I responded quietly.

"Ah," the man's wife said, "isn't he so cute?"

"Leave the boy alone," her husband retorted. "Where did you learn to play like that?"

"Here."

They all laughed when I said that.

A slightly shorter and stockier man asked, "So how long have you been playing, then?"

"A few days."

They all burst out laughing again.

"Really?" he asked. "Or is that what that guy told you to tell everyone?"

"No," I said, "I swear."

"I'm sorry," the stockier man said apologetically. "Either way, you played a great game. You flew the flag for Persia high."

The first man's wife had been itching to talk and asked quickly, "Is it true you are here alone, Sweetness?"

I didn't want to answer, but as everyone was looking at me, I nodded.

"Ah, you poor baby," she said. "Are you doing okay?"

"I'm fine, thank you," I said. "I'm sorry, but I have to go now. It was a pleasure meeting you all."

Like a rehearsed choir, they all replied, "You too. Goodbye!"

As I left, I could hear the woman's husband scolding her. "You scared him," he said. "Couldn't you leave the poor boy alone?"

"What did I do?" I heard her say.

At reception, the last of the crowd was leaving. Murat came toward me. "Little Man!" he exclaimed with his arms open.

"What?" I said brusquely. I could not keep my feelings hidden. I was angry and it showed.

"You played a great game, Little Man." He tried to hug me, but I shrugged him off.

"What is it, Little Man?"

"I might be young, but I am not stupid, Murat."

"What do you mean?"

"Okay," I said, "how much money did we win?"

"Well," he said, "that is a good question. Around ten thousand lira."

"Yeah, right."

"What do you mean?" he asked, looking offended.

"I am not stupid, Murat," I shouted. "I am not doing this any longer."

143

"What?"

"You heard me. You keep trying to cheat me."

"No, I don't," he said, dropping his voice lower. "How was I trying to cheat you?"

"You thought the fat guy was better than me, but you told your friends that I was good. Then you gave them good betting odds on me to win, thinking that I would lose. Then if I lost, you would keep all their money, and I wouldn't know the difference. You would walk away with all of it."

"But—"

I did not let him talk. "What's more, if I had lost, I would have felt guilty and upset that I had let you down."

I paused. The silence was thick between us.

"Little Man—"

"Little Man nothing!" I said. "You lied—again."

I began to walk away but he stopped me. "I'm sorry."

"Yeah? Again?"

"I would have given you your cut of the money."

"Sure you would have."

"I swear."

I just laughed at him. "You know what?"

"What?" he asked.

"How do you know that the fat guy was not working with one of the guys who bet on me, and didn't throw the game?"

"Oh . . ."

"Yeah," I said, "you didn't think of that, did you, when you didn't back me?"

"No."

"Well, you'll never know that, will you?"

"I'm so sorry, Little Man. I've learned my lesson now."

"Sure. Whatever."

"Really, please forgive me."

"I forgive you, but I am not playing again."

"What? You *have* to. I need to make my money back."

"Not my problem."

"Listen, what can I do to make this up to you?"

I looked at him, aghast. I was really surprised at his audacity. Then I realized that this was an opportunity for me. I could lay down my own terms.

"Well, how much money did you lose?"

"A hundred and fifty thousand."

"Okay, you have to give me five percent of that, for a start."

"What?" he screamed in shock. "But I lost!"

"What's another seven and a half thousand lira when you've lost a hundred and fifty thousand already?" I asked. "Besides, you don't have to pay in cash. You can take it off my bill."

"Suppose I do that," he said and then asked warily, "What else?"

"For a start, you *always* have to bet on me, and there will be no running of books on my games unless you tell me."

"Okay, what else?"

"You always tell me the amount I'm playing for before the game, and I want to see the money."

"Done."

"One more thing."

"What now?"

"I want a job."

"You *what?*" He couldn't believe his ears.

"I want to work in the hotel on the days that I have nothing to do."

"First of all," Murat said slowly, "I have no money to take anyone on, and if I did, he couldn't just choose his own days."

"I can," I said. "I've thought about it."

"Oh, and how does that work? I take it off your bill again?"

"Well, that's an option, but I was thinking of something else."

Murat stared at me open-mouthed.

"I've just seen a lot of your Iranian guests," I started to explain, "and they all love me."

"Even if you say so yourself!"

"Well, they do."

"Okay, so what if they do?"

I dropped my voice to a whisper. "Well, they feel kind of sorry for me—at least their wives always do."

"Get to the point."

"Hold on," I said. "You see, I can be the tea boy. If I am the one selling the tea, they will order more and give me tips as well. You will make more money with better sales, and I will make extra money with my tips."

Murat stared at me as if I had suddenly sprung two horns.

"Are you really only nine?"

"Nearly ten."

He shook his head incredulously. "It sounds good," he said, "but I'm agreeing only on a temporary basis to see if it works."

"Fine."

"But if I want you to play backgammon, that will have to take priority."

"And I choose my own hours."

"Done."

"So you're taking seven and a half thousand off my bill?"

"Ye-e-s-ssss."

"I have it all written down, you know."

"Oh," he said with a chuckle, "I would expect nothing less."

I had to buy food before it got dark, so I headed for the corner shop. I was in a good mood. I had gotten everything I'd wanted from the backgammon situation. It was obvious that Murat needed me more than I needed him. This made negotiating with him easy. I was pretty proud of myself.

I entered the shop, and this time the smell of the kavurma was too tempting. I decided that I deserved some meat after two days of bread and yogurt.

The shopkeeper recognized me immediately. "Kavurma today, Little Man?"

"Yes," I responded, "it's Friday."

He grinned to himself as he took great care over his toasted masterpiece. He handed it to me in a bag along with the loaf of bread, the two bottles of water, and the pot of yogurt I had picked up, and in his broken Farsi he said, "Enjoy, Little Man."

When I returned to the hotel, the sun was about to set. It was early yet, but I went to my room to relish every crumb of my delicious kavurma. I was always hungry now. I tried to eat as slowly as possible to make it last longer.

I wondered if my parents would call that night. My father had promised that he would, but I was not sure anymore. I thought of telling them about my new job. Even though I felt my father had let me down, I yearned for his respect.

After my dinner, I ran down the stinky stairs and took my position in the lounge. It was beginning to fill up, with everyone returning after the day's business. I decided that it was a good time to start working. I went to reception only to find Murat feeling sorry for himself.

"Murat?"

"No more conditions. You're killing me."

"No, I just wanted to know where to write down the guests' tea tabs."

"Oh," he said in a surprised tone, "you're starting now?"

"When better than the present?"

"Very funny, Little Man," he said. "You know what your problem is?"

"No, what?"

"You don't act your age."

"But I'm only nine."

"I know. That's my point. It's scary. You should try acting nine rather than a hundred and nine."

I laughed. "Okay," I said, "but where do I write down the tabs?"

"I'll show you," he said with a sigh. He led me through the corridor and took me behind the bar. "Okay," he said, "you see this list?"

"Yeah."

"Just write what they order next to their room number."

"So, not just tea?"

"It's evening now. Not everyone will want tea," he said.

"Okay," I said, a little unsure.

"If you're uncertain about anything, come and ask."

Everyone in the lounge was looking at us. Murat noticed this, and like the fox that he was, he decided to announce my new position.

"Ladies and Gentlemen," he declared, "may I introduce our new barman and tea boy."

He pointed to me and they all began to clap. I glared at Murat, who said quickly, "And may I also add that he only earns the tips that you may wish to give him."

I kicked Murat on the shin when he said that, because it made me look desperate, but I was also happy that he had done it, because now I did not have to say it myself.

"Good luck, Little Man." Murat went back to his throne, and I was left in charge of the bar.

There was a little pause before the lady from that afternoon waved me over. I went to her, and she patted my head.

"You are so cute," she said. "I want to take you home with me."

I smiled at her and hoped that she also wanted to order some drinks. Unfortunately, she did not, so I asked her, "Can I get you a drink, Madam?"

"Ah, he's so polite, too," she told her husband.

"Can't you just leave the boy alone? He's not a toy."

"Yes, I want to order a drink." She had pleased me at last. She was a kind lady, but at this point I just wanted to make money.

"I want tea and so does he." She pointed to her husband.

"No, I don't," he snapped. "I want a beer."

"Okay."

I went to the kitchen, poured the tea, and got some sugar cubes and a teaspoon, which I placed on the saucer next to the small glass of tea. Then I went to the bar and opened the fridge. I saw quite a few different types of beer, so I chose the brand I had seen people drink the most. I took the drinks over to the couple but did not wait to be tipped, as I was too embarrassed. I waited to be called back by the lady, but it was the man who spoke. "Hey, Kid?"

"Yes, Sir?" I walked back to him, and he gave me a hundred lira.

It was not a huge amount of money, but I had not expected that much. As I walked back to the bar, I worked out that if

I served twenty drinks and got similar tips, it would pay one-third of a night's stay.

I had forgotten to ask for their room number, so I went back and approached the lady, since I was intimidated by the man.

"Excuse me, Madam?"

"Yes, Sweetness?"

"What is your room number, so that I can put the drinks on your tab?"

"Thirty-seven."

"Thank you, Madam."

I saw her gesture to another couple, indicating that I was adorable.

Another man called out to me, "A beer for me too, please, Kiddo, and don't worry about the glass. Room twelve."

I liked such people. He was trying to make my life as easy as possible. He had a 150 waiting for me!

Then the orders began to come thick and fast, until I was rushed off my feet. The guests in the lounge were competing with each other in typical Iranian fashion. Instead of keeping the tip at a hundred lira, they were all trying to outdo each other with higher tips, until I reached my largest tip of the night—350 lira! This seemed ridiculous, but I wasn't complaining. Murat would be happy, as he was selling a lot of drinks, too, and he made good money on those.

"Abbas!" It was a while later when I heard Murat come in and shout, "You've got a phone call."

"Oh," I said, "can you take over for me until I get back?"

"Sure."

I put my tray down and ran toward the lobby. I had been so busy that I had completely forgotten about my parents.

"Maman?"

"Abbas." My father's deep voice echoed down the line. "It's me."

"Is Maman there? Can I speak to her today?"

"No, Son," he said, "not today."

"Why not?" I demanded.

"Because I say so." That was that.

There was silence as I waited to hear what he had to say. "I'm sorry I did not call yesterday, Abs, but . . ."

"It's okay."

"Yes. Listen, your mother is really worried about you, and I don't want her to be more anxious."

"I'm fine. I'll tell her that, Baba. I promise."

"I know, I just don't think that . . ."

"Have I ever told you that it's horrible here? Have I not done everything that you told me to do?"

"Yes, but it's not that simple, Abs."

There was another pause. I did not know what to say to him, and he was not saying what I wanted to hear.

"So how are you, Abs?"

"I'm okay," I said, trying to hold back my tears. "Things are going well. I wrote a few letters to Maman, and I watch a lot of television, and I don't leave the hotel unless I have to—just like you told me to."

"Good lad."

"So do you know when I will get my papers?"

"I sent them all together today by express mail, so they should be with you within five to ten days. That is what the man at the post office said."

"Okay," I said despondently. "So when will I be able to speak to Maman?"

"Soon."

"Fine, Baba. Go before your bill gets huge."

"Yes," he said and then fell silent for what seemed like hours. "You take care, Son."

"Bye, Bab—"

But he had hung up the phone.

I sat on the stool and wiped my tears before peering around the corner to make sure no one had seen me. Then I ran into the kitchen and washed my face.

Murat came in with a tray of empty glasses. "What did you do to these people? They are ordering like there's no tomorrow."

I smiled. I needed a bit of good news.

"You've got the job for as long as you want it."

"Thanks."

"This is great business, Little Man. You're even more clever than I thought."

"I know."

"Modest, too."

I chuckled.

"You'd better get back out there before they start protesting."

"Okay." I was halfway out the door when Murat called me back.

"Little Man?"

"Yes?"

"Some of the guests were keen that you got this," he said, handing me a wad of notes. It was the tips that I had not collected yet. My bundle was quite thick now.

"Little Man? Good job."

I was ready for bed. It was well past three in the morning. That night I was so tired that, before I knew it, I was fast asleep.

Ten

From the moment I opened my eyes, I knew that this day was different from all the ones before it. I did not know why, but the sun was shining, the noises from the street were far below their usual alarming level, and for the first time, I had a smile on my face at the beginning of the day.

Until today, I had been just as wary of boredom as anything else. Now I knew that I had things to do: a letter to write, backgammon to play, and tea to serve when I felt like it. As I was getting dressed, I noticed that even the scurrying cockroaches did not horrify me anymore.

Of course, I knew that there were people who would not hesitate to take advantage of me. Even the person I had thought of as my closest ally had tried to do that. I knew I was still very vulnerable, but at least I now felt more secure in my surroundings.

Before going downstairs, I took stock of how much money I had. I had written down what Murat owed me on a small notepad. Most of my money was still unspent, but I did not have all that much in lira. I decided to take another trip to the town center and check what rate I could get.

I was looking forward to seeing Hector. He had been good to me, though I had learned from my experience with Murat that I could not always blindly trust those who were nice to me, so I made up my mind to compare rates before going to Hector's shop, just in case.

Murat was on duty, half-asleep in his usual way behind the reception counter. He handed me paper, pen, and envelope automatically, and despite my happier mood, I began the gloomiest of my letters since I had left Tehran.

Dear Maman,

I hope you are well. Days are passing by slowly. I am still waiting for the papers that Baba has sent. I'm fine, but I cannot help but feel a little sad because I have not spoken to you in a very long time. Every time I ask Baba, he tells me that I can speak to you the next time, and it does not happen. Do not worry about me. I just would like to speak to you, that's all.

I really miss you.

Your son, Abbas

When I put the envelope on the counter, Murat reached over to the backgammon board. I put my hand out to say no.

"A champion needs to practice," Murat said, waking up.

"Yes, but a champion also needs to have lira."

"Ah," he said, "I can swap money for you."

"No," I said. "I have a contact in town who gives me the best rate."

"Oh, really? And who is that?"

"Just a friend," I said with a smile. "His name is Hector."

"Hector, huh?" he said with that suspicious smile of his. "And what rate did he give you last time?"

"A thousand."

Murat did not respond for a few seconds. After careful deliberation, he asked, "What about the tea?"

"What about it?"

"Well, someone has to serve it."

"I don't think my customers will be up anytime soon. They went to bed too late."

"*Your* customers are they now, eh?" he asked.

"You know what I mean."

"Yes," he said, laughing, "I'm just teasing. But seriously, what if someone does want tea?"

"Then someone else has to do it, because I will be out until lunchtime," I said, shrugging. "Besides, the agreement was that I choose my own hours."

"I guess we did make that arrangement," Murat said, defeated, only to raise his voice again in excitement as he thought of something new: "But we did also say you are working on a trial basis!"

"First you said that. But later you said I have the job for as long as I want."

"I said that?" he asked. "The problem with you is—"

"That I don't act my age. I know!"

"That too," he said with a chuckle, "but I was going to say your memory is very good."

"That means I have two big problems now."

"I guess it does," he said, smiling. "Now off with you. The sooner you go, the sooner you will return."

My good mood changed immediately once I stepped outside. I needed to get out every now and again for my own sanity, but I didn't feel comfortable alone on those streets. The farther I walked from the hotel, the more crowded the streets became. The main street that led to the market was so busy I could not see beyond five feet.

My intention was to go into the market, pass Hector's shop without being detected, and get three or four rates from different shops. Then I'd return to Hector's and decide what to do. On getting my lira, I would go straight back to the hotel.

As always, things did not quite pan out the way I had envisioned.

I managed to find my way through the jostling crowds, and I arrived at the market gates in very little time, with my suspicion that everyone wanted to mug me probably making me go faster. I stopped at the gates and decided to think about how I was going to pass Hector's shop. The likelihood of my being seen by him was low, but I wanted to make sure.

A group of American tourists was gathering next to me, and their guide began to lead them inside. This was perfect camouflage. No one would bother me, as they would think that I was with my parents. It worked.

I went from jeweler to jeweler. Once again I was getting a standard rate of 980 lira everywhere. Finally, I walked hesitantly toward Hector's shop. He bounced to the door and opened it for me.

"Abbas, my friend," he said, "welcome back."

"Thank you."

"Please, please, come in, my friend," he said with the respect that one pays a king. "Pepsi or Fanta?"

"Sorry?"

"What would you like to drink? Pepsi or—"

"Really, Hector," I said, "I've just come for—"

"Today's rate, right?" He was so enthusiastic that it was almost abnormal.

"That's right."

"I'll give you one thousand, one hundred lira per dollar, and I'll guarantee—"

"I'll take it," I said before he could finish.

"That was easy. What is it? Are you no longer cautious?"

"It's not that," I said, grinning. "I have already checked what everyone else is offering."

"You're a clever one," he said with a smile. "I told you that before."

"I'll exchange fifty dollars, please."

"Sure," he said seriously, "but please, have a drink with me first." I looked at my watch and saw that I had plenty of time to get back for the lunchtime rush at the hotel. I did not want to lose out on my lunch-hour tips.

"Okay," I said. "I'll have a Fanta, please."

"Fanta coming up."

Hector was about to go and get it when I said, "Sorry, Hector?"

"Yes?" He turned with a smile.

"How much will that be?"

"What? The Fanta?" he asked in astonishment.

"Yes," I said, feeling embarrassed at having asked.

"My friend," he proclaimed, "you are my guest. It is free, of course."

"Oh," I sighed, blushing, "I see. I'm sorry, Hector. You know . . . I . . ."

A look of sadness appeared in his deep-brown eyes. He stood motionless, looking at me for what seemed like an eternity. I looked down. "I'm sorry if I said anything, sir, that—"

"It's not you, my child." There was a pause as he chose his words carefully. This was the first time someone had addressed me like that since my Turkish adventure had begun. I liked "Little Man" more, but there was affection and caring in Hector's words. "It's so tragic that our world today breeds such cynicism in children."

"Oh," I said, pretending I understood what he was talking

about. I sat on a little stool in the shop, and soon he came back with a Fanta. I took a sip and, looking down, I noticed a hole in the crotch of my jeans!

I tried to hide the hole, and I was so preoccupied with it that I stopped listening to what Hector was saying. Suddenly, I was in a hurry to leave the shop. I drank in big gulps. Then Hector said something that completely changed the events of that day.

"Abbas," he said thoughtfully, "I was going to ask you if you wanted a small job once or twice a week—but I don't want to do that anymore."

"What job?" I asked.

"No, really," he said, "it doesn't matter." Of course, the more he protested, the more my curiosity grew. I should have known better . . .

"No, tell me. What is it?"

"It's nothing," he said. "A simple job."

"*What?*" I demanded.

"All you'd have to do," he explained in a casual manner, "is to take a parcel half a mile to another shop, down the same road your bus left from the other day."

"What's in the parcel?" I asked.

"That I cannot tell you," he said sharply. "You would not be allowed to open the parcel, either."

"How much?"

"Twenty US dollars."

"What's the catch?"

"There isn't one," he said. "It's just a confidential delivery, that's all."

This was too good to turn down. "So how big is this parcel? Is it heavy?"

"God, no," he said with a smile. "Look." He got out a parcel from behind the counter. It was about twelve inches square and four inches high.

"I'll do it."

"What, now?"

"When better than the present?" I was sure that Murat would have chuckled at my using "his" phrase.

"Are you sure?"

"Yes," I said excitedly, "but I get paid now, right?"

"No," he explained. "I'll give you ten dollars now, and the man you will deliver it to will give you another ten when he receives the parcel."

"Okay."

"Good," he said. "You take that road where you got on the bus. Walk about five hundred yards up that little hill and along the row of shops on the right-hand side of the road. You'll come to a launderette."

"Fine."

"There you will see a very large man. His name is Adil," he said. "Give the parcel only to him. One more thing . . ."

"What?" I asked.

"If you think anyone is watching you or following you, do

not under any circumstances go to the launderette. Do you understand?"

"Yes," I said, but now I was a little frightened. "Why would anyone do that?"

"I'm just warning you."

"Oh," I said, pretending to understand even though it did not make any sense. I didn't mention it again, because twenty dollars was a lot of money to me. "So if anyone does follow me, do I bring the parcel back here?"

"No!" he said, almost having a heart attack. He then returned to the counter and got a little card out. "Take this card," he ordered, "and if that does happen, go to your hotel and ring me on this number. Okay? I will tell you what to do and give you the rest of your money then."

"That sounds fair. So do I have to report back here if it is delivered?"

"No," he said calmly, "just go home."

"But how will you know that I did deliver the parcel?"

"That is a good question, Abbas," he said with a smile. "Your proof is the ten-dollar bill that he will give to you."

"But that could be any ten-dollar bill," I said. I was not that stupid. "What if I want to spend it?"

"The bill will have something written on it in pencil in a corner," he explained. "You can spend my bill, and then next week, if we repeat this, I'll give you another bill in exchange for the penciled one, plus the ten for next week's delivery."

"So I only get half of my money this week?"

"No, you get all of it," he said, "but if you want your proof, you can't spend half for one week. That's all."

"Okay," I said as I thought about what he had said. "So can I have my ten dollars?"

"Sure," he replied. With that, he pulled out the biggest bundle of dollars I had ever seen. He had every denomination possible. He must have had at least five or ten thousand dollars. I was impressed.

I took my money and the parcel and made my way through the bustling crowds. I knew that it must be valuable; otherwise he would not be paying me so much. I knew, too, deep down, that what I was doing was wrong, but the temptation of the money was too much. I did not know how long I would have to stay in Istanbul and support myself. What I knew for sure was that, of all my jobs, this was the one that my father should never find out about. My other two jobs were good, but they did not pay anywhere close to this one. This was easy money, but my mother's old proverb rang inside my head: easy money was the Devil's money.

As I walked up the small hill, I kept turning around in case anyone was following me. I was walking very fast, my heart was racing, and I was sweating heavily. All of a sudden, it did not seem such a good idea to be doing this, but it was too late now.

Before long, I noticed a dingy, dark little launderette. I looked back one final time and then crossed the road so I was

directly opposite the launderette. I walked twenty yards farther, crossed the road again, and went back. I looked through
the window, but it was so dark that I could not see the far
side of the shop. I pushed the door slightly and immediately
jumped as a bell jangled. I could not imagine anyone using
this launderette to wash clothes. Mold covered the walls and it
stank of cigarette smoke. The floor was sticky, and as I walked
across, it squelched. My heart was beating even faster now.

As I walked through the thick smoke, I saw someone who
fitted the description of Adil. He must have weighed more
than three hundred pounds. He was back behind a counter
lying in a plump leather chair that had its stuffing bursting out
of several holes. He had a badly misshapen nose, undoubt-
edly broken several times. His old-fashioned mustache curled
at the ends, and he had heavy stubble and shaggy sideburns
in need of a trim. He was dripping sweat, despite a little fan
whirling in front of him. I could see rolls of flab popping out
of his tight, yellow, cotton shirt. I was terrified as he stared at
me.

"Excuse me, sir?" I inquired in Farsi in my faintest and polit-
est of voices. "Are you Adil?"

"Uh-huh," he grunted.

"I have this for you." I offered the parcel.

He took it very gently from my hands, and then with great
effort he stood up from his seat. Big drops of sweat snaked
down his face as he glared at me and then looked at the parcel.
"Wait."

He disappeared through the back door, then came back and leaned forward over the counter. My heart stopped. I thought he was going to hurt me. Instead, he opened his hand and offered me a ten-dollar bill. I took it from him, and sure enough, there was a five-digit number written in one corner. Adil was staring at me, but I seemed to be paralyzed. I just stood there.

"What else do you want? A kiss?" His voice echoed in the dank, moldy space.

"Oh, sorry," I stuttered. "I mean, thank you. Thank you, sir." I backed out the door, keeping Adil in sight. As soon as I was out of his range of vision, I began to run. I had my twenty dollars, and it had been worth it. After all, it had only been forty-five minutes of work. That was more than my father would earn in that amount of time.

I started to make my way back to the hotel as quickly as I could, since I was already late for lunchtime and my tips. I was gloating.

Suddenly, a heavy blow smacked across my chest. I was knocked to the ground. A man had been walking fast in my direction, and because my head was lowered, I had not gotten out of his way. The man was furious, towering over me and shouting in Turkish.

I tried to apologize. "I'm sorry, sir," I said.

As soon as he heard me speaking Farsi, he became even angrier. He leaned over and pulled me up by one of my ears.

He said something about Iranians, but I could not understand it. I guessed it was not very pleasant. Then, out of
nowhere, he slapped me right across the face. Hate welled
up inside me as never before. Then he spat on my head and
walked away.

Passers-by had stopped to watch, and yet no one had bothered to help me.

As soon as I got up and away, I checked my pockets for my
money. It was all there. Then I felt the man's saliva begin to
drip down my forehead. I pulled the end of my sleeves over
my hands and wiped his spit from my head.

As I turned off the main road onto the street for the hotel,
my face was stinging, but something inside me hurt more—
humiliation, and the pain of feeling like an outsider. Trying
to work out these things by myself was confusing, but who
could I confide in? I knew I couldn't tell my parents. Their feelings of guilt would only be multiplied.

It was past one in the afternoon when I finally stepped back
into the hotel. I was trying to focus on the next task at hand.
Murat was in his seat, waiting like a parent whose child had
missed curfew.

"What time do you call this?"

"I told you earlier," I snapped, "the agreement was that
I choose my own hours. Besides, I said I would be back by
lunchtime, and it *is* lunchtime."

"Hey," he said, taken aback by my abruptness. "I was only
joking, Abbas."

"Sorry," I said softly. "I'll need ten minutes before I can start."

Murat stared at me. "Sure, take your time," he said, walking toward me. He reached out to touch my face gently. I wanted to flinch but stood my ground. He tilted my head to one side.

"What happened to your face?"

"What do you mean?" I asked, pretending innocence.

"It's completely red on one side," he said. "What happened?"

"Nothing," I responded with my head down.

"Did someone hit you?"

"No."

"Then what happened?" he demanded. "Was it when you were swapping money?"

"No, I got my money," I said. "I got one thousand one hundred lira per dollar." But I wasn't gloating anymore. I was desperately trying to think of something I could say to avoid further interrogation. I could not possibly allow Murat to know that I had been hit, that I was vulnerable. The image I had always given him had been one of a smart boy who knew exactly what he was doing.

"Okay," he said, "but I know that something did happen."

I walked quickly out of the lobby and up the stairs. All I wanted to do was get into the shower. I washed my hair five times with shampoo. I wanted to remove all traces of that man.

A knock at my door made me jump. I ignored it.

After a few seconds, there was another tap. I heard Murat. "Little Man?" he called. "Little Man, are you there?"

"Yeah," I responded, "hold on." I finished dressing quickly and then opened the door a chink.

Murat was there with a bag of ice, which he handed to me. "Keep that on your face for twenty minutes or so. It will reduce the swelling."

"Thank you."

"Little Man," he said thoughtfully, "you don't have to tell me what happened, but if you do want to . . . well, I am here."

"Thank you."

"Make sure you keep it on for at least twenty minutes, and then come downstairs. There are a lot of thirsty Iranians waiting for you."

"Okay," I said with a slight smile.

I could not figure out Murat. I still did not know whether to trust him. He would make incredibly kind gestures and then try to pull a trick on me. Perhaps he was nice to me only because he was looking after his investment.

When I returned downstairs, I immediately went to work. I smiled when I had to, and it appeared that my fame had spread across the hotel. Everyone knew who I was. I learned to remember little details about each of the guests, because they liked me all the more for it. I always asked them how their business was going. They would tell me about their children, and I'd write down the names of their kids on the tab list so that I would remember, should I serve them again. Murat loved the idea and began to use it himself.

However, throughout the whole day, I hoped that my parents would not call. I was sure I'd break down on the phone, and that would be the end of that. I did not eat. I drank lots of tea, played a game of backgammon, and served drinks until two in the morning. My parents did not call, and I was as happy as I was sad about that.

After the bar closed that night, I went to my usual seat in the back row of the lounge and stared at the television until I fell asleep. I did not want to go to bed, even though I was exhausted. I woke up around three and finally decided that I should go upstairs. When I climbed into bed, I prayed to God that when I woke I would not remember what had happened to me that day.

Eleven

The next two days were dark. As hard as I tried to forget, the memory of that slap on the face would not leave me. To add to that, my parents had not called me for three days in a row. I know I could have called them, but I did not want to anger my father by spending the money.

I had left the hotel only once since that eventful afternoon, to buy some bread, cheese, yogurt, and water. I thought I deserved a little cheese, considering my new earnings. I had played three games of backgammon and maintained my one hundred percent victory record. Murat's bets were no longer as high as they had been earlier, and that took the pressure off me. I continued to serve tea with considerable success. It was the one activity that took my mind off my problems.

I now had a second nickname. Due to my slightly bruised face from the attack, some of the hotel guests had begun to call me Rocky. I have to say that I was quite partial to that name. Rocky was my hero! That movie was one of the first American films I had ever seen. Most of the pirated movies that came into Iran were from Bollywood, but occasionally, the major Hollywood hits also sneaked through.

When I woke up the following day, I made my way straight to the kitchen for some tea. Murat was up and looking unusually bright. He was dressed neatly and had even bothered to apply aftershave. He strolled in with a smile.

"Little Man, I have some good news for you."

"A raise?"

"Good try, but no," he said with his cheeky smile.

"Then what?"

"Someone has a letter today."

"Who, me?"

"Yes, you," he quipped.

"Where? Where?" I asked enthusiastically.

"On my desk," he said, following me. I was already halfway there. I could see the red *Express* stamp on the airmail envelope. I ripped it open to find the documents I had asked for, all held together with a paperclip. On top was a letter from my mother.

"Your documents?" Murat asked.

"Uh-huh," I said, half ignoring him as I took the letter and the papers to my little corner in the lobby. I was almost too scared to read the letter. It had been so long since I had heard from my mother. This was the closest I had been to her since my departure. The fact that she had written the letter with her own hand, the fact that I recognized the paper as the kind she always wrote on, and best of all, the fact that the letter still smelled of her perfume, made me happy. Really happy. I began to read.

My darling Abbas,

How are you, Azizam? You cannot imagine how much I miss you, my boy. The house does not feel the same. I keep feeling that you are here or thinking that I see you. I even think that I can hear you some afternoons, playing with your friends outside. I go out to see Suroosh, Farhad, Paima, and the rest of them playing soccer. I look for you, but I can't find you. My life is not the same without you. I am sorry that I cannot speak to you on the phone, but your father does not think it is good for either of us at the moment. However, he has promised me that we will talk soon.

You do not know how proud I am of you, Abbas. You were my little boy only a few days ago, and now you are a man on your own. No one else could do what you are doing, my boy, but you can, because you are special. I cannot imagine how hard it must be for you. Just be strong a little longer. Pray to God, and you will see that He will answer you. I pray for you every night, Abbas, just as I taught you to do.

I will not tell you all the things that you have to do, because I know you are doing them already. I know my boy.

I am more sorry that I had to let you go at the airport than I am about anything else in my life. I am trying my hardest to join you, my child. If you are ever sad and think that life is hard, remember that you are not alone, and that I am thinking

*of you. Whatever happens, remember that I am really proud
of you.*

I love you more than anything else in the world.

Your mother, Marzieh

*P.S. Mamanjoon sends her love and says that she misses
you dearly.*

I must have read that letter ten times. In Iran, I had always
been embarrassed when my mother had shown me affection,
but now I would have done anything to see her and tell her I
loved her. I was so happy and sad at the same time. To read
that someone was proud of me put a real smile on my face.
At the same time I wanted to cry, because I missed my mother
more than anything in the world. Murat could see that I was
in an emotional state. To his credit, he stayed in his seat and
let me get on with it.

I still had plenty of time to get to the consulate, but first
I had to get changed into something smart. I returned to my
room and dug out all of my clothes, only to realize that I was
nearly out of clean ones. I would have to do some washing
soon, but I managed to put a respectable outfit together in a
hurry.

I was tired of carrying all my money on me everywhere I
went. I needed to find somewhere safe for it. The cleaning girl
was young and looked trustworthy, but I had to check for myself. I left a fifty-dollar note in plain sight on my bedside cabinet and pinned another to the bottom of my mattress. I might

lose a hundred dollars this way, which was a lot of money, but it was better to lose a hundred than a thousand. I wanted to see if I could trust the cleaner.

I walked downstairs past a few guests who greeted me with their usual, "Hey there, Rocky!" or "Ah, isn't it a shame for a boy to be on his own." Some people thought that, just because I was young, I was also deaf. It had stopped bothering me. The advantages that it brought far outweighed the disadvantages.

As soon as Murat saw me, he knew I was going out. "When will you be back?" he called.

"I don't know," I replied. "I am going to the consulate. Why?"

"Well, I wanted to know if you'd be here for tea, and . . ."

"Have you got a match lined up?" I asked, guessing where this was going.

"Well, kind of," he responded, "but it's not definite."

"I should be back by the evening for sure." I was at the door when Murat called me back.

"Little Man?"

"Yeah?"

"Good luck."

Outside, I was of two minds about whether to keep my head down or to look ahead. If I did the latter, I thought I might make myself more of a target, so I tried to settle for a compromise between the two. I think I must have looked mighty silly with my head going up and down like a yo-yo. Once on the main road, I noticed my heart beating faster. As I walked past the spot where I had been attacked, I gritted my teeth and decided that the best way to deal with this was to walk briskly.

I made it to the bus stop without getting into trouble. It put me in a good mood. I was convinced there would be a major breakthrough at the consulate today. Because I had my papers, I was sure they would issue me a visa instantly.

I waited for the bus for about twenty minutes. I was getting quite impatient when I noticed a lady next to me, a Persian. She could not have been more than twenty-five years old and was very beautiful, with long, thick black hair and deep brown eyes. She looked at me but clearly thought twice about talking to me. Curiosity must have finally gotten the best of her, though, for after a few minutes she spoke.

"Excuse me?" she asked politely in a delicate voice.

"Me?" I asked, pointing to myself, though I knew she was talking to me as she was speaking Farsi, and besides, there was no one else there.

"Yes," she said with an elegant smile, "you. Are you Persian?"

"Yes."

"Oh, good," she said, relieved. "I'm here alone, and it's good to see another Persian."

"I know what you mean."

"Where is your mother?"

"In Tehran."

"Oh," she said. "You're here with your father?"

"No, I'm alone."

She hesitated. She thought she had misunderstood. "Sorry?"

"It's okay," I said like a seasoned professional. "I am alone without my parents, and I'm fine. Honest."

She smiled, thinking I was pulling her leg.

"Really," I said, "I'm going to the British Consulate. I'm waiting for the bus."

"Oh, thank God," she said with a sigh of relief. "So this is the right stop for the British Embassy?"

"Actually, it's the consulate," I said.

"Oh, right," she said, surprised I would know the difference. "Yes, that's what I meant."

"It's fine," I said, trying to reassure her. "I made the same mistake."

There was a pause. "So does the bus stop outside the embassy?" She saw me look at her. "I mean, consulate."

"Yes," I said, "but listen, do you speak English?"

"I do. Well, a little, anyway."

"Okay," I said to her, with my cheeky smile, "I'll make you a deal."

"What?"

"I'll take you to the consulate and show you how it all works if you will translate for me when we get there."

"I don't see why not," she said. "So you know how to get a bus ticket and everything?"

"I do," I declared in my know-it-all manner. "Do you have a hundred-lira note?"

"I think so."

"Then you don't need a ticket," I informed her. "Just put the money in the machine. It works like a ticket."

"It does?"

"Yup."

She was suitably impressed with my knowledge. "What's your name?"

"Abbas, but some people call me Rocky or Little Man."

"They do?" she said, smiling. "Well, I'll call you Abbas. I'm Tarineh."

The bus came soon after, and we sat together and chatted all the way. I told Tarineh about my situation, because she was going to find out anyway while interpreting for me. Then she told me about hers. The poor lady had left Iran to try for a British visa so that she could escape the regime and live with her aunt in London. She desperately wanted a visa because otherwise her family would force her to marry a Persian man another aunt had found for her. She told me that she did not love him, and it would not be right. She looked so sad that I felt really sorry for her. I was realizing that every person in Istanbul had a story.

As we approached the consulate gates, I noticed that one of the armed guards from my previous visit was there. It was clear he recognized me, so I walked ahead of Tarineh, who was digging in her handbag for her papers. I didn't even have to show him my passport. The guard just let me in with a wave. I waited for Tarineh inside the consulate gate.

"Do you know them?" she asked as she joined me.

"Kind of," I said. "We met on my last visit." I kept it short, because I did not want her to know I'd had to cry like a baby to be allowed in.

We walked silently up that magnificent drive toward the consulate door. Tarineh was trying to absorb it all, just as I had on my first visit. As we entered, we separated into the lines— one for men and one for women.

Judging by my ticket number, it seemed like I had an hour's wait. I looked along the cubicles, and sure enough, the serious-looking interviewer from my previous visit was there at his usual counter. He noticed me and gave me a little nod. I realized that even this little gesture must be unusual for him.

Eventually, Tarineh came through and sat next to me.

"They certainly search you properly, don't they?"

I nodded and asked, "What's your number?"

She showed me her ticket.

"I think you're about twenty minutes after me," I said.

"Will that be enough time for your interview?"

"I don't know," I said, suddenly feeling a little uneasy. "I hope so. If not, then you go and have your own interview."

"Okay."

We sat together for about forty minutes and talked about anything and everything. I was quite surprised at the things she told me, even about her boyfriend back in Shiraz who she had almost married, but then he ran off with another woman! I was beginning to realize that marriage in Iran was a compli-cated business.

Eventually, the number before mine flashed on the screen. I was next. We waited for about five minutes and then the number *after* mine flashed. It had skipped my number!

What should I do? I jumped up to go check, but my serious-looking friend started waving to me from his cubicle, gesturing to me to sit down.

"What's happening?" Tarineh asked in a hushed voice.

"I think that man over there wants to see me," I said, pointing to him.

A few minutes later my number flashed, and when I looked over, I saw my friend's counter was vacant. Tarineh and I walked over to it, and the man smiled at me.

"You're back, I see," he said to me as Tarineh began translating.

"I have brought the documents you asked for," I said to the man and Tarineh simultaneously.

The man nodded and then examined my papers. After about five minutes of inspection, he looked back up. "Good," he said. "You've brought everything I asked for."

"Does that mean I can have my visa now?"

Tarineh looked at me in a funny way. Then, as she translated, the man began to laugh.

"What's so funny?" I asked, a little put out.

"It's not quite that simple," the man said, still laughing. "Come back between two and three o'clock in exactly ten days. It is important you come at the time that I have asked you to."

Once Tarineh had translated his instructions, I looked up at the man. "Thank you," I said in English. My over-optimism had revealed my immaturity, and I felt a little stupid, especially after the way I had tried to portray myself to Tarineh as someone who knew how to navigate the consulate. I learned something that day.

The man kept my papers, shook my hand, and that was the end of my consulate visit.

Tarineh still had a wait.

"I'll stay, and we can go back together, if you like," I offered.

"Are you sure?"

"Yes."

"Thank you," she said, smiling.

When she came back from her own interview, we walked out of the building without speaking. Once we were on the drive, I looked up at her. "How did it go?"

"At the moment," she said with sad eyes, "it looks like I'm going to be marrying that guy my family wants me to marry."

"Why? What happened?"

"God knows," she sighed. "They want a million different papers."

"They did for me, too," I explained. "That's normal, I think."

We chatted a little on the bus, but it was obvious that her mind was somewhere else. We got off by the marketplace. As we were waiting to cross the road, Tarineh took my hand. When we reached the other side, there was an awkward silence.

"So then, Abbas," she said with a forced smile, "I guess this is it."

"Yeah."

"Will you be okay?"

"I have been so far," I murmured. "Will you be all right?"

"I think so," she said, "though I have a few things to learn about this place, and you won't be around to show me."

I wanted to tell her where my hotel was and say that I'd be glad to help her again, but even though my instincts were telling me good things about Tarineh, I knew I needed to be cautious.

"It's not all that hard," I told her. "You'll be fine."

She leaned over and kissed my cheeks. Then she spent a few seconds wiping her kisses off. I turned very red.

"Good luck with everything, Tarineh," I whispered.

"To you, too, Abbas," she sighed. "To you, too."

She turned and was about to walk away when I called after her. "Tarineh?"

"Yes?" She smiled as she turned.

"I hope you don't have to marry that man."

She patted my cheek without saying anything and then left. I watched her disappear into the crowd.

I was close to Hector's shop and decided to go in and see him. He came through the back door and gave me a huge smile.

"Abbas, my friend," he said, "great job the other day."

"Thanks," I muttered. Before I knew it, Hector was hugging me and kissing me on each cheek. It made me feel uncomfortable.

"One minute," he said as he ran out back. I sat on the little stool in his shop and waited. Hector returned with a bottle of cold Fanta and offered it to me.

"Thank you," I said, downing it in a few gulps. I was thirsty after my day at the consulate. Hector watched me, grinning the whole time.

"I see you were thirsty, my friend."

"Yes," I said, catching my breath, "I haven't had anything to drink all day."

There was a pause as I decided on the best way to approach the subject. "Hector?"

"Yes?"

"I was just wondering," I said, "when my next delivery will be. . ."

"Ah," he said, "I should think in about three days."

"Okay, I will be back in three days, then."

"Great."

"Thank you for the Fanta."

"My pleasure," he said, smiling. "Oh, by the way, do you want me to swap your ten-dollar note?"

"Um . . ." I stuttered, "no . . . no, thanks. It's at home, and I didn't know I was coming here today. I will bring it when I come next time."

"As you wish."

"Thank you, though."

He waved me off. I actually did have the ten-dollar note

with me, but all my money was together in one wad, and I did not want Hector to see the rest.

On the way back to the hotel, I started to worry about the other money I had left in my room. I began to kick myself. If that money was gone, I would never, ever be able to tell my father.

Entering the hotel, I saw Murat on the phone. He tried to stop me, but I ran past him and up to my room. The fifty-dollar note was on the bedside table right where I had left it—now with the room's ashtray on top of it to stop it from flying away. Imagine my happiness! And sure enough, the other note was still pinned to the bottom of the mattress, too.

I sat on my bed, smiling to myself, and thought about getting some provisions. As I was about to leave, I had second thoughts. If the money was still there, did that mean that the room was safe, or were they trying to trick me into leaving more money behind? I decided to play on.

I hid a note under the insole of one of the pairs of sneakers I had left in the cupboard. Then I decided to use a trick I had seen in a Bollywood film: using some Blu Tack adhesive, I stuck two hundred-dollar bills to the top of the drawer inside the bedside cabinet, so the drawer itself would look empty if someone opened it. Also, there was only a slight gap, barely big enough for my hands, between the bottom of the cup-board and the floor. The cupboard was very heavy. I blu-tacked two more bills to the bottom of the cupboard, as far back as I could reach. Right then and there, I decided that it was stupid to carry all my money in one pocket. I split the rest of the money and put just one hundred in my trouser pockets, then divided the rest between my underpants and my socks. Then I went to get something to eat.

On my way back from the corner shop, I saw a small boy with a portable shoeshine kit. I had seen many such children in the marketplace. They charged a hundred liras to shine a pair of shoes and sat on little stools, usually against a wall, with their boxes in front of them. There was a foothold on their toolbox where the customers rested their feet while the children cleaned their shoes. This gave me an idea, but I decided to keep it to myself for the moment.

I ate in my room, and lonely though it was, it was nothing like it had been earlier. I still looked at my family pictures and missed them all, but it was gradually beginning to sink in that I would not see them for a long time.

After dinner, I went downstairs and got to work on the tea and the bar. I was getting quite familiar with all the liquors. I only really got confused with "mixers" for drinks, but only Westerners ordered them, and there were only a handful of them staying here. These would be the less affluent business-men who could not afford the hotels where other Westerners stayed. They had fancy names for their drinks, which entailed putting lemonade or Coke in with the alcohol. I didn't like these guys so much, because they were stingy with their tips. The few English people I had met in Istanbul had not made a great impression on me, and I could not help but judge the whole nation by them.

I was behind the bar when Murat came in and gestured that I had a phone call. I ran to my usual booth and took a deep breath, praying that I would hear my mother's voice.

"Hello?"

"Abbas?" My father's voice echoed down the crackling line.

"Oh," I sighed, "hi."

"How are you?"

"Is Maman there?"

"She is asleep."

"When can I speak to her?" I asked. "I promise not to upset her, Baba."

"I know, my son," he said. "I promise you—and I have never broken a promise to you, right?"

After a brief pause, I said, "Right."

"Well, I promise," he went on, "that the next time I call, you'll speak to her."

"All right."

"So how are you?"

"I'm okay," I said. "I got the documents this morning."

"You did?" he exclaimed. "I was going to ask."

"Yeah, they came all intact, and I got the letter from Maman."

"Good."

"Thank her for me, please."

"She says thanks, too. She got two letters from you today."

Immediately I felt better. I had been wondering if they'd gotten there yet.

"This is what I want you to do, Abbas," my father went on in a serious tone. "Tomorrow, I want you to go back to the consulate with all the documents and—"

"Baba?" I tried to cut in.

"Go with the documents, and—" He spoke louder, over my words.

"Baba!" I said even more loudly.

"What is it?" he snapped. "I'm trying to tell you what to do."

"Well, it's just that I have already been to the consulate."

"I know, but you have to go again with the documents."

"I have."

"When?"

"Today."

"How could you have?" he asked. "You said that you got them today."

"I did," I declared, "this morning. I went there immediately."

"You did *what*?" he asked. "Why didn't you wait for me to tell you what to do?"

"Because I knew what to do," I said quietly. I was afraid that he was going to shout again. "The man at the consulate had said that I should go back when I had the documents."

"That's true, but you should have waited for me to call in case I had some instructions for you."

"I know, Baba," I said, "but you had not called for several

days, and I didn't know when you would. I just want to get this done quickly so that I can get out of this . . ." I paused.

"This what?" he asked in a hushed tone.

I didn't answer the question, and a silence filled the air as my father considered his next question. "This *what*, Abbas?"

"Nothing, Baba," I said. "It's just that I don't know how long my money will last, so I tried to get things done quicker."

He could not argue with that.

"It's okay, Abs," he said. "You did what you thought was best. No, you did well, actually. You took the initiative, and that is great, Abbas."

"Thank you," I said, half-smiling. I don't know if my father had suddenly remembered that I was only nine, or if he actually believed I had done well.

"So what happened?"

"Well," I said enthusiastically, "I saw the same man, and he was pleased that I had all the papers he had asked for."

"He was?"

"I think so," I went on, "and he told me that I should go back in exactly ten days between two and three o'clock. What does that mean, Baba?"

"I don't know, Son," he said, "but let us hope it means something good. I will call you again before you go back to the consulate."

"When, Baba?"

"I don't know, Abbas, but soon," he muttered. "Now, you only go out when you have to."

"I know."

"Goodbye then, Abs."

"You won't forget your promise, will you?"

"No, Son. No, I won't."

"Thank you. Okay, Baba, goodbye."

That conversation had been the best I'd had with my father since I arrived in Istanbul. It was also the first one I'd had without crying. That really put me in a good mood for the rest of the evening, which I spent serving drinks.

That night, I slept with the lights on as usual, looking at my family photographs, but inside I was feeling better. Thoughts of that man hitting me popped into my head once in a while, but it didn't get me down as it had earlier. A few warm words from my father had made such a difference.

TWELVE

Four more days passed. I made one more delivery for Hector without incident. He had given me a new ten-dollar bill plus my money for making the drop. That was the only time I left the hotel, except for routine trips to buy food.

Even though I was beginning to cry less and was able to get on with things, I woke on the fifth morning feeling miserable. There was good reason. I stayed in bed and waited for the sun to rise. As I lay silently, I began to think about my first night in that very same room. All the noises were suddenly louder in my ears: the dripping taps, the random bystanders who made their way on the street below, and of course, the insects that inhabited the room with me. I managed to get a few more hours of sleep before I woke again around eight o'clock.

I walked down the stairs to find Murat half-asleep as usual. I had not written a letter home since my last conversation with my father five days earlier. I walked straight to Murat's desk and, after a halfhearted wave, helped myself to paper and a pen.

"Help yourself," he quipped, "why don't you?"

"Thanks," I said. He smiled a little before dozing off again. I knew that I had certainly improved business for Murat since my induction as the tea boy. I slipped into my usual spot on the dingy old sofa and thought hard about what to write.

Dear Maman,

How are you? I am doing well. In five days, I am to go back to the consulate. I have given them all my documents, and they are checking them. I have learned how to make time pass, but I never stop thinking of you.

Today I am ten, and no one here knows. It is the first birthday that I have had without you or my friends. I remember you telling me how lucky I was to receive gifts, when I did not like one of my presents a few years ago. I know that now. I don't want any presents this year; I just want to see you. Baba promised that the next time he calls we can speak to each other. I have not heard from him in five days. I woke up early this morning wondering if you would call me today.

I hope you will, but I won't mind if you can't, Maman. I haven't forgotten that you have nothing back in Tehran. When we left for the airport, the house was empty. You'll join me soon anyway, so you don't have to put up with that much longer. I'm sure Baba will sort everything out and buy more things. He always seems to manage somehow.

If you and Baba had left Iran before the revolution, when we were rich, maybe we would all be together right now. I do a lot of thinking here. I have a lot of time to myself. In Tehran, I was always out playing soccer or riding my bike. Here I have no friends, so instead, I think. My money is lasting well. I am eating only once a day and not spending money on anything silly. Everyone here knows me now. Most people here are Iranian, and I am almost famous among them. Most of them are really good to me. One of the ladies who was staying here actually looked like you. I didn't speak to her, though. She only stayed a day or two.

I guess I had better go now, but I am thinking of you, Maman, especially today.

Lots of love,

Your son, Abbas

I folded the paper over, walked to the reception area, and sealed it in an envelope. I wrote the address on it very quietly in order not to wake up Murat, but he startled me with, "It's okay, I'm awake."

"You are?"

"I have been for a while." He yawned. "I just like to rest my eyes."

There was a pause as I played with my letter. It must have been obvious that I had something on my mind.

"What is it?" he asked. "Spill it out."

"Nothing . . . Well, actually, there is something—"

He cut me short with, "No, you can't have a pay raise."

"No, it's not that. I was just wondering . . . You know those children who shine shoes on the street?"

"Yeah?"

"I was thinking that I could do that."

"I wouldn't recommend it," he said very simply. "You shouldn't go on the streets. Those children belong to gangs and you'll get hurt."

"Oh," I sighed, "but I don't want to go out there. I thought we could do it here."

"We? Here?" he parroted, puzzled.

"Yeah," I went on more enthusiastically, "why not? Everyone here is either on business or trying to get visas. They all have to look smart. We could have the box here in the lobby, and in the morning, if their shoes need a polish, they could get it done on the way to the embassies or their meetings."

"You've been thinking again, huh?"

"Also, we can do it like the Hilton in Tehran. My father told me that when he used to stay there, they would polish shoes at night and leave them outside the door for you."

"He did, did he?" he asked.

"Yeah," I said, smiling, "and guess what? We could charge more for that!"

"You crack me up," he said, laughing loudly.

"So?"

"So what?"

"So what do you think?" I asked.

"Well," he said, stuttering, "I don't know. Have you not got enough jobs here?"

"I still have a lot of free time."

"So if—and that is a *big* if—I say yes to this crazy idea, how do we do this?"

"Well, I was thinking . . ."

"Oh, no." He slapped his forehead. "I don't like it when you think."

"Very funny. I was thinking that if you buy the equipment, which by the way, I have seen in the market, we could go fifty-fifty."

"How does that work?" he asked. "I'll be the one paying for the equipment."

"Yes," I said, "but the idea is mine, and I will be doing the work, too."

"Yes, but you'll be using my lobby," he argued.

"That is why you're getting fifty percent, for the money to buy the equipment and the use of your lobby."

"What happens when you leave?"

"Who will serve tea when I leave?"

"Someone else."

"Well, there you go."

He knew it was a good idea needing only a very small investment. After fifty or sixty pairs of shoes, he would earn his money back and start to make a profit. He also knew that not many other inexpensive hotels offered the same service.

"Okay," he said, "I'll see what I can do."

"Cool," I said, smiling. "And you can't go wrong, because I'll take the money and give you your half."

"You're something else."

"I know," I said with my cheeky smile. "Oh, and Murat?"

"What now?"

"Get a good box and a stool."

"Okay, go away now," he said. "You're getting sassy."

Happily, I walked off to the kitchen to get my morning glass of tea. I had expected Murat to at least put up a fight on the percentage. It had been easier than I'd thought. I had managed to get my fourth job in half as many weeks. It was a good start to my birthday.

The day was pretty humdrum. I played a few games of backgammon with Murat just for fun, and I served a few glasses of tea, but it was not until nighttime that it got a little more interesting.

I had not seen Murat since four o'clock. I had been working behind the bar in the television lounge, and the later it got the more upset I became, as my parents still had not called me. The lounge was filling up fast, and I was getting busy. All the Persians were there, ordering their usual drinks, and the tips were pretty good. My parents, however, monopolized my thoughts, and nothing was going to change that.

Suddenly, Murat flew into the lounge and waved at me. I indicated that I was really busy and could not leave the bar immediately. He kept beckoning me insistently. I thought this meant that I had a phone call, so I dropped everything and ran to him.

"I have a surprise for you, Little Man."

"What?" I asked. "A call?"

"No," he said. "Why? Are you expecting one?"

I shook my head. "No."

We walked to the lobby. "This, Little Man, is better than any call."

"I doubt it."

"Yes," he said, "just wait and see." And with that, he revealed a really large and glamorous shoe-cleaning box and stool. The box had brass handles, a beautifully made wooden frame, and drawers. It came with all the supplies. The little stool was covered with purple velvet. I was impressed, but I just shrugged.

"What?" he asked. "I thought this is what you asked for."

"It is," I said halfheartedly.

"It's one of the best out there," he carried on. "My friend gave it to me for a good price."

"Great."

"You don't like it?"

"Yes," I said, "it's really nice. We'll do well with it."

"That's what I like to hear," he said proudly. "Try it out."

I sat on the stool, which was against the wall near the entrance to the lobby. It felt quite comfortable. I started to look through all the little drawers and compartments. Murat put his foot on the box with a smile.

"Let's see how good you are then, Little Man."

I looked up at him and did not say anything. I really did not want to clean his shoes. To begin with, he was not paying. More importantly, I suddenly realized the first pair of shoes that I would shine signified an all-time low for me. Though I was brought up without the trappings of nobility, I was always told to behave as if I was an aristocrat. This shoe-shining business had been my idea, but when it came right down to it, I had not imagined I would feel this bad doing it.

I took out the brush and the brown polish and began to smear it all over his shoe. Then I picked up the shining cloth and began to put my back into it. Murat stood there watching. I was not going to let on that I was upset.

After five minutes, I had finished both his shoes. He inspected them, turning his feet up, down, and sideways. Then he smiled his usual cocky smile. "Not bad at all. You just need to be a bit quicker."

He started to whistle as he walked off to the kitchen. I sat alone in the lobby, thinking about the fact that it was my birthday and my parents had not called. I wanted to cry. How long would I have to live like this? I was trying to make the most of the experience, but it was affecting me deeply.

Suddenly, I felt a thud on my box. It was one of the Persian guests who had been staying at the hotel for a while. He always tipped me well when I served him tea.

"Can you do mine?" he asked.

"Sure."

I began to work, and he watched me in silence. I tried to be quicker than when I had cleaned Murat's shoes. The gentleman was pleased with my work and paid me my hundred liras plus a tip. I put the tip in my pocket and put the hundred in one of the drawers, which I had decided to use as a till.

For the rest of the evening, I went back and forth from the kitchen to the bar and back to my box. A lot of people were having their shoes polished that night just because of the novelty of it. Murat had put up a sign in the reception area for an overnight shoe-cleaning service at a rather high charge of 250 liras.

There were new guests in the hotel that day, a Persian family, and they had a little boy who was about my age. I had heard him crying earlier because his mother had not bought him the chocolates he wanted. I had laughed to myself on seeing that, for not too long ago, I might have behaved the same way.

I was sitting at the box, counting the money I'd earned when the boy approached me with a hundred-lira note. He put his foot on the box.

This, for me, was the ultimate humiliation. After the first time that night, I had not minded cleaning the shoes of people older than me, but I found it difficult to cope with this. I picked up the brush and began to dip it into the polish.

As I was about to put the brush to the boy's shoes, Murat called from reception, "Hey, Little Man, phone call!"

Without even looking at my customer, I dropped everything and ran to the booth. "Hello?"

"My darling baby," my mother said. "Happy birthday, Azizam." Her voice was soft and gentle, and I could feel her love for me in every syllable she uttered.

"Maman? I miss you so much," I sobbed. Yet I was thrilled.

"I miss you too, my darling," she said. "It's just not the same here without you."

"Sometimes I think that you've forgotten about me. I thought Baba might call more often."

"He wants to, but . . ." She paused, and I knew why. My father must have been next to her.

"Baba is there, isn't he?"

"Yes."

"Is it because we can't afford to speak too often?"

"Yes, Abbas," she said. "That is the only reason."

"Are you crying, Maman?"

"No, of course not," she said, trying to hide her sadness.

"Don't cry, Maman," I said. "I'm fine here. I can take care of myself. Don't worry about me. I am doing fine."

"I know, Azizam," she said. "We are so proud of you. We all are."

"You are?"

"Of course," she said. "Do you think just any boy could do what you are doing?"

"I don't know," I said.

"Well, they couldn't," she said firmly, "and even if you weren't doing as well as you are, I'd be proud of you."

"Thank you."

"Abbas?"

"Yes?"

"I'm so sorry that I can't be there for your birthday. I know it must be lonely for you."

"Don't worry, Maman," I said. "I got my birthday present by speaking to you. I also have the letter that you sent with the papers."

"Baba told me you liked it."

"I loved it," I said. "Send me more, please."

"You know I will."

"Does Baba want to speak to me?"

"Yes, he does, my darling," she said, "but before I forget, Mamanjoon sends her love."

"Say hi for me. Go now, Maman. I don't want the bill to get too high."

"Okay, baby. I love you."

"I love you too, Maman."

There was a slight pause as my father took the receiver from my mother. I knew that now I had to compose myself. I had to give the impression that I was in total control.

"Abbas?"

"Hi, Baba," I replied in my merriest tone.

"How are you, my boy?"

"Good, thank you, and you?"

"Can't complain," my father said with his gentle humor. "Happy birthday."

"Thank you, Baba."

"You're a man now?"

"I guess."

"If you like, you can buy yourself some chocolate or something," he said. "Sorry that we can't be there . . . or give you gifts."

"It's okay, Baba," I responded. "I don't want chocolate, anyway. Besides, it's dark outside, and I don't want to leave the hotel."

"Good boy," he said, "but if you want chocolate tomorrow, it will still be okay."

"Thank you, Baba, but I don't think I will."

"So?" he asked. "What are you doing tonight?"

"Oh, nothing," I said as I looked at my smudgy hands. "I'll probably watch some television. You go now, Baba. It's late over there."

"Okay, Abbas," he sighed. "You take care of yourself, and I'll call you the night of your consulate trip."

"Okay."

The phone clicked, and I knew that it would be another five days before I spoke to either of them again.

I came back and found the boy still waiting next to the shoe-shine box.

"Sorry," I said. Speaking to my mother had given me strength, and I was ready to get my hands dirty.

"What is your name?" the boy asked.

I looked up at him. "Abbas," I told him brusquely, hoping that would be the end of the conversation.

"Do you not want to know what my name is?" he asked.

I didn't, but I couldn't say that. "Sure."

"Amir," he said. "My name is Amir."

"Hi," I said.

"Hi," he replied. "We're here to get a visa for America. I can't wait to get there. My father says they have amazing toys."

I wanted to laugh. Now I understood what Murat meant when he said that I had to learn to shine faster. It was for my own sake. I had not talked to anyone my age for a long time, and my patience was running out with this one.

The rest of the night I was busy working in the television lounge, serving drinks. Usually, I would have stayed downstairs in front of the television until I was sleepy. However, on that night, I was eager to go to my room. I lay on the bed and stared at my family pictures.

I did not cry. I simply fell asleep.

Thirteen

During the next four days, I tried to occupy myself with as much work as I possibly could. The only incident worth reporting was that I lost my first match in backgammon. It was close, but I was outplayed by a better player. Luckily, Murat had not put a lot of money on me, as he knew that I was the weaker player. I think he had hoped for a miracle.

The shoeshine business was doing very well, and to annoy me, Murat kept commenting on how it had all been his idea. I'd always point out that he had to trust me to give him his fair share of the money, and he would smile. He never tried to check whether I was stealing from him, and of course I didn't. I did not share the tips with him, so I always made more than him anyway.

I was not in top form, because my birthday was still at the back of my mind. My mother's voice had been a reminder of what I was missing by being in Istanbul.

The day finally arrived when I had to go back to the

consulate. I came downstairs in my best clothes and gave my own shoes a good shine. In the same way I could drink free tea, I could polish my shoes for free, too!

I had decided this was the day when I'd take a risk. "Murat," I said. "Do you have some of the lira I asked you to put in the safe for me?"

"I have all of it," he said with a smile. "Do you want it?"

"Yes, please."

Without hesitation, he opened the safe, and there was my pile. It had built up slowly as I had added my earnings to it.

I took the liras. "Murat?"

"Yes?"

"Can you put some of my dollars in there?"

"Sure," he said, "how many?"

"Around eight hundred," I said softly. He looked at me very coolly and winked.

"No problem, Little Man."

He took the money from me, put it in an envelope, and wrote my name on it. Then he put it in the safe where my Turkish liras had been. I just did not want to worry anymore about losing the money. I had four or five hundred dollars more hidden in my room and the rest on me. I began to walk off to the kitchen to get some tea when Murat stopped me.

"Oh, by the way, are you going to write a letter today?"

"No," I said. "I will speak to my parents tonight."

He had started to get on my case because I had stopped writing as many letters as I used to. It was nice of him to do that. He said that it was important to write letters to one's folks. Murat's own parents lived in a village a long way from Istanbul, and he had told me that ever since I had arrived, he had started to write to them.

As I sipped my tea, I wondered what was going to happen at the consulate. I hoped that I would be as lucky as I was on my last two visits in finding someone to translate for me. I wondered if I would see Tarineh there. I knew that it wasn't likely, but it was possible, as she, too, had been asked to return with her papers in ten days.

I got off the bus outside the consulate. Both the armed guards from my first visit were there, and with gentle smiles they opened the gates again without looking at my passport.

It was a really busy day there. I could not see a single empty seat. Now I was less worried about finding a translator and more worried about how long I'd have to wait.

As I went toward the ticket machine to take a number, a series of loud taps stopped me. They were coming from the booth of my friend. He was waving at me like a crazy baboon. I could not understand what he wanted me to do. He began to point to a door behind the glass booths, which only the consulate staff used, so I started to walk toward it. I saw the man smile from behind his counter. The more he smiled, the faster I walked.

I stood at the door, waiting. Almost everyone in the consulate was now staring at me and obviously whispering about me under their breath. I was beginning to panic. Who would translate for me?

The door opened, and my friend guided me through with a welcoming gesture. Behind the booths was a fantastically air-conditioned, open-plan office with computers and photocopying machines. The desks were all immaculate, and the people working there were dressed in elegant business clothes. The carpet looked soft and fresh, as if it had been shampooed only the day before. There was a rosy smell of air freshener.

I followed the man through another door at the back of that office, which led to a long corridor with polished floorboards instead of carpeting. There was a heavy wooden bench outside imposing oak doors in the center of the corridor. At the far end, I could see the entrance to a grand foyer. The man indicated that I should sit on the bench and wait. He spoke, too, but I only understood the gestures. I sat staring around me. There were huge paintings, larger than me, of horses and foxes, hanging on either side of the wooden doors. These oil paintings were like none I had ever seen before.

I must have waited for over an hour. I did not see anyone at all in that time, and I began to panic that they had forgotten about me. Suddenly, a man who looked very Persian appeared and walked toward me. He smiled at me but did not say anything.

The man knocked on the large doors next to the bench, and a loud, resonant voice responded, "Enter."

The man went in, and once again I waited alone. Then the

door opened. A man of considerable stature and class stood before me. Immediately, I rose to my feet. He had blond hair that was turning white, and the wrinkles in his skin gave him the look of a wise man. His small, piercing blue eyes looked out from behind delicate, metal-framed glasses, and he was dressed in a finely tailored beige suit, a salmon-pink shirt, and a silk tie with a perfect knot. He offered his hand.

"Hello," he said in a deep voice.

As I understood, I responded in English. "Hello, my name is Abbas Kazerooni."

The man chuckled, then made a remark to the other man who had entered the room before me. I could not understand what he said, but they both laughed. The Persian-looking man also came up to me and shook my hand.

"Hello, Abbas," he said in Farsi. "I am a translator. They were expecting you, and they asked me to come in and help you."

"Thank you," I said in English.

I was still completely awed by this magnificent office. There were old school photos on the walls and more oil paintings and souvenirs from all over the world. There were photographs of the distinguished-looking man with the Prime Minister of England, Margaret Thatcher. I knew who she was because my father always talked about her. He would tell me how Margaret Thatcher was tough and would tolerate no nonsense.

On a mahogany desk lay fancy fountain pens and beautifully framed photos of what must have been the man's family.

The man in the beige suit gestured to me to sit down, and he turned to examine a sheaf of papers. I recognized some of them as the documents I had given to my consulate friend ten days before. He then spoke very quickly and firmly to the translator, who made a few notes and then turned to me. "This, Abbas," he said, "is the man in charge of the consulate. He is a very important man, the consul."

"I can tell."

"He does not usually get personally involved in visa cases, but on hearing your story, he decided to look at it himself."

"Thank you," I said, again in English. This was making the man smile. It was the core of my ten-word English vocabulary.

"He says it is important that you do not lie about anything, because that would mean that you will never get a visa for England."

"I know. I told the other man only the truth," I said firmly.

The translator and the consul exchanged a few more sentences before the translator turned to me again. As he was about to speak, a lady knocked on a side door to the office and walked in carrying a tray. On it was a glass of water, hot chocolate in a fine china cup, and biscuits. She gave the water to the translator and then set down the tray in front of me. I did not touch anything.

"The consul says that it is all for you," he said, smiling. "He says it is his son's favorite."

With that, the consul picked up one of the photographs

on his desk and showed me a picture of his wife and his son. Hesitantly, I picked up the cup, making sure I did not spill any of it. It was delicious, and I downed it in a few gulps.

Then the translator got us back to business. "The consul says that he knows you have told the truth so far, as your story has been verified. He just wants to caution you for the future."

"Okay."

"He says that he wanted to meet you, and he is pleased that he has. He says that he likes you."

"Thank you." Again I spoke in English to the consul. He nodded at me.

The translator continued, "He wants to help you, but he cannot guarantee anything. Do you have any questions?"

I thought about it before answering him. "Yes. I want to know how long these things take."

The men conferred for a few minutes, and then the translator told me, "The consul says that there is no set timeline for these things, and he cannot give you a specific date, because he does not want to disappoint you. However, he does say that he has a boy very close in age to you, and he knows that he would not want him to be alone in Istanbul. He says that he will try his best for you, but again, he wants you to know that there is no surety. After a point, it's not in his hands."

"Thank you very much," I said to the consul.

He smiled at me again, and from his eyes, I could tell that he did genuinely like me.

"So what should I do now?" I asked.

"You have to go now and come back in six weeks," the translator said.

"*Six* weeks?" I was horrified.

"Yes, I'm afraid so," he said. "This is the day you should come back." He handed me a piece of paper with a date and time written on it.

"I will be here again to translate for you," he continued. "They have the hotel details in case they need to get in touch with you before that."

"Thank you."

Both men stood up, and I immediately stood, too. The consul walked up to me and shook my hand again and said something to the translator.

"The consul says to look after yourself, and he hopes to see you soon."

"Thank you."

With that, the consul accompanied me to the door, where a lady was waiting to take me back to the main consulate area. As I left, I took one last look at the splendid room.

Walking out of the consulate, I did not know whether to be happy or sad. I had to wait six weeks, but the most important man in that consulate had taken a liking to me. I stood waiting for the bus, famished and wanting to get back to the hotel. There was only about an hour of sunlight left when the bus arrived.

In the meantime, I was thinking about how my father would react when I told him what had taken place. He might order me to return to Iran and try to save the rest of his money. It made my head ache to think of all the different scenarios that each day brought with it.

By the time the bus dropped me off by the marketplace, it was almost dark. The street to my hotel was unlit. I had never walked it in the dark before and it scared me. In my room, I could hear all sorts of noises coming from the street, but now, as I walked along, it seemed terribly silent. The only lights that lit my way now and then were from the few houses and flats.

Finally, I spied my hotel and decided to make a dash for it. I landed on the steps, panting. To my great surprise, I saw Murat in my place behind the box, cleaning someone's shoes. He was much too big for the child-sized stool, and I laughed at him as I walked through the door.

"Oy, where are you going?" he asked. "Don't you want to carry on for me?"

"No, I have to go and get some food first."

"What about when *I* get hungry?" he asked. "Do you see me leave my post to go and get food?"

"No." I said, darting out of the lobby anyway. I hurried up to my room, changed my clothes, and checked to make sure that my money was still there. Then I took a few hundred liras with me and returned downstairs. As I did, I saw Murat walking out of the kitchen. He burst out laughing.

"What?" I asked.

"Your jeans." I looked down at them and noticed that they looked a little odd.

"I don't understand."

"You are not the first," he said knowingly, "and you certainly won't be the last."

"What?"

"When you washed your jeans, you didn't rub them together hard enough. That means that the lighter parts are cleaner than the darker parts."

"Oh," I said. I felt a little stupid, but to be honest, I was more interested in getting something to eat than worrying about my pants.

I had just walked out of the lobby when Murat chased after me. "Phone call, Abbas," he screamed.

"Already?" I asked as I ran to the booth.

"Abbas," my father said, "how did it go?"

"Hi, Baba," I said. "Oh, well, it went fine, I think."

"What happened?"

"Well, I met with the guy in charge of the consulate."

"The ambassador?"

"I think so," I said. "They called him something else. Apparently, he does not usually get involved in these kinds of cases."

"Why did he meet you?"

"Because he wanted to see me for himself, and he likes me. He said that he will try to help me if he can."

"That is great news."

"But he said that there is no guarantee," I explained, "and that I have to go back in six weeks."

"Six weeks?"

"He said it takes time," I said, "but if they get any news before then, they will call me at the hotel."

"But, Abbas, what are you going to do for six weeks on your own in Istanbul?"

"I've been here almost three weeks already, Baba," I said. "I'll be okay. Besides, the man said that he has a son my age, and he doesn't like the thought of me here alone, so he will try his best for me."

"He said that?"

"Yes."

"How did you speak to him?"

"He had a translator for me."

"Great, they got a translator for you! That is good news."

"So I will just wait it out."

"We'll see."

I did not know what he meant by that, but I was almost hoping he would tell me to come back to Tehran.

"Is Maman there?"

"Yes, hold on." His response took me by surprise.

"Hello, my darling. How are you?"

"I'm good, Maman," I said, all cheered up. "How are you?"

"Missing my baby."

"Maman!" I said, almost blushing.

"My man, sorry," she corrected herself.

"Yes, I went to the consulate and saw the most important man there. He said he would try to help me."

"I heard, Sweetness," she said proudly. "Well done!"

She'd said exactly what I wanted to hear her say.

"Thank you, Maman."

"Abbas," she said, "what do you do with your time when you are not at the consulate?"

Had she guessed I was up to something?

"I watch a lot of television and play backgammon."

"You do, huh? Well, you take care of yourself, Abbas. Don't you get into any trouble because you have a lot of time on your hands now."

"I won't, Maman. I'll be careful."

"Good boy," she said. "I know you will."

"Well, you better go. The bill will shoot up."

"We'll ring again soon," she said. The phone clicked.

When I came out of the booth, I saw that Murat was not at the reception. I presumed that he was in the kitchen or in the television lounge. I did not really want to leave the hotel, but it had been more than twenty-four hours since I'd last had a meal. I decided to walk as briskly as I could to the corner shop.

The street seemed ghostly, a wind whistling ominously down it. Deep inside, I felt something was wrong. However, by now I was more than halfway to the shop, and I thought I should carry on. The only thing that I could see was the light of the corner shop.

Out of nowhere, an arm reached out, held me by the neck, and pulled me into a narrow, dark alleyway. I froze, terrified. A thin, sharp-looking man with a heavy cloak or blanket over his shoulder smacked my head hard against the wall and held a knife to my throat. He had small, beady eyes. As he breathed heavily into my face, the stink of alcohol made me feel sick. He whispered in Turkish and kept showing me a small bag.

"I'm sorry," I whispered, "this is all I have." I opened up my hands to reveal around 250 lira, which was nothing. Either the fact that I did not understand him or that I did not have money angered him. His voice began to get louder. I kept repeating, "This is all I have," in Farsi, and he seemed to get more and more aggravated. Still holding the knife to my throat, he began to search my pockets. When he found nothing, he got even more frustrated.

He picked me up and threw me against the opposite wall of the alley. My head hurt from this second pounding. He followed me, held me by the neck, and again pressed the knife hard against my throat. I was shaking and looking up at him when he suddenly punched me across my cheekbone.

I was sure I was going to die. I closed my eyes and felt the knife blade going in a little deeper. All I could think about was that I didn't want to die here, in this unfamiliar city, down a dark alley where my parents would never find me.

My eyes were still closed when, out of nowhere, my name echoed down the alley.

"Abbas? Abbas? Abbas?"

I was sure I was imagining it, but when I opened my eyes, there was Murat. For a few seconds, my attacker stared at him. Murat stood his ground. Then the attacker turned and ran down the alley. Immediately, I got up, pretending I was okay, but my heart was racing a thousand miles an hour.

I stumbled into the street. Murat reached out to gently touch my shoulder and then my neck. It was not a deep cut, but blood was dripping from it. My head was aching, too, and as I touched it, I realized that the back of my head was bleeding as well. Tears were streaming down my cheeks.

"Are you all right?" Murat asked. I saw him stare at my jeans. I had wet myself from fear.

I could only nod. If I had spoken, I would have become hysterical. This was the only time Murat ever saw me cry, but he behaved like a true gentleman.

"It's okay, Little Man," he said softly. "Tell me what you wanted from the shop and I will get it for you." I shook my head to indicate I didn't want anything.

"You go back," he said. "I know what you eat. I'll get it now."

I nodded to say thank you. As I turned around, he called to me again. "Little Man?"

"Yes?" I sobbed.

"Don't worry. No one will know about this unless you want them to." He stood there and watched me walk all the way to the hotel, then turned and walked down the alley to the shop for me.

In those few minutes, I had experienced the two extremes of life: evil and good.

As I approached the lobby, I checked to make sure there was no one there and then ran up to my room. I did not want anyone else to see me in that state. I could not believe how close I had come to death.

I wanted to be home now more than ever.

I wanted to give up.

I had tried my hardest, but it just wasn't good enough.

I thought about calling Baba. This had been a stupid idea, and my father should have known better than to send me to a city like Istanbul alone.

I cried as I took off my clothes. My neck was bleeding a lot worse than my head, even though my head was hurting more. I stood in the shower and stared at myself in the mirror. The left side of my face was swollen. *What have I done to deserve this?* I kept thinking to myself. After my shower, I decided, I would call home.

I sat in my pajamas on the side of my bed, not knowing what to do. My neck had stopped bleeding, but my head was still hurting. There was a knock at the door.

I did not respond until Murat called out, "Abbas, it's me." I opened the door and let him in.

"Here," he said, "I've got some bread, cheese, yogurt, water, Coke, and some chocolate for you."

I did not want to argue with him over what I did or didn't want, so I reached for my money on the bedside cabinet.

"Don't be silly," he said softly, "it's on me."

"No," I said, "take it."

"Don't make me throw you out of my hotel," Murat said with a smile.

"Thank you," I said, "for everything."

"It's nothing," he said. "Oh here, this is for you, too." He held out some ice. "Put it on your head and face. Do you need to see a doctor?"

"No," I said firmly.

"Okay," he said. "Do you need anything else?"

"No, thank you."

God must have been watching me that night. I knew that Murat never left the hotel on his shift; but this time, he told me, he had run out of cigarettes, and he did not have anyone to fetch them for him. So he had gone out while I had been on the phone. On his way back, he had come upon the attacker and me.

"You rest well," he said, "and if you want anything, just let me know." Murat left and I was alone once again. I locked the door and stared at the food. I could not eat anything. When that man had slapped me in the marketplace, I had thought it could not get any worse, but it had. I sat on the bed crying for what seemed like hours. I eventually found myself half-asleep on the floor.

I was glad that my parents had not called, because I could not have controlled myself. I decided that I was not going to tell them. They would only blame themselves.

I woke up the next morning around four o'clock, a nightmare about the previous night making my head spin and hurt. I could not go back to sleep, but I did not get up. When the cleaner knocked on the door, I did not let her come in. I stayed in bed and stared at the wall. I did not want to speak to anyone. And there was no way I had the energy to work. Murat did come and speak to me through the door, but I told him that I wanted to rest. By the end of that day, I ate a little bread, which made me feel a little better.

For three days I stayed in my room, away from the outside world. The only reason I decided to go out again was because I thought I would run out of money if I stopped working. The swelling on my face had gone down somewhat, and my head was not pounding as much as it had been. I promised myself that I would go downstairs the following morning.

FOURTEEN

I t was early morning. I edged my way past the curtains and opened the window for the first time since I had arrived. With a creak, it let in a fresh, chill breeze. I sat on the edge of my bed and watched the sun make its way above the buildings across the road.

I was dreading seeing Murat. I felt humiliated and embarrassed, though he had been an angel. I went downstairs and walked into the deserted lobby to find him in deep sleep at his desk. I got myself a glass of tea and went into the television lounge. There were a lot of empty glasses and ashtrays from the previous night. This was not really my job, but I set to work picking them up and cleaning them.

I heard Murat walk in. "You know you won't get paid any extra for that?" he said jokingly.

I smiled at him. "I know, but I needed something to do."

"Why don't you write a letter home?" he asked.

I was not sure that I could cope with writing home and not saying anything about what had happened, but I nodded.

"Good," Murat said. "Besides, I have a match for you today. You'd better practice."

"So should he," I said, trying to make the atmosphere a little lighter. I began to walk back toward reception, then stopped to ask, "Are the paper and the envelopes . . . ?"

"Where they always are," he confirmed. For a man who did not have children, he showed great patience with me. The more I got to know Murat, the more I realized what a good man he was.

I returned to the lobby and stared at the paper for a long time without writing anything. Eventually, I began.

Dear Maman,

I hope you are well. I am doing all right. It has been pretty boring since my consulate visit. I have watched a lot of television and slept a lot. It was so good to speak to you, though, Maman. I wish you could have been here with me. Maybe while I am killing time before I go to the consulate again, you can sort out your papers and join me. I could show you how everything works here. I know before I left I never used to tell you how much I love you, but if I saw you again, I would not be embarrassed, even if my friends were there!

So how is Mamanjoon? Is she still up to her old tricks? Tell her I miss her, too. Tell her now that I am ten. I am a real man!

Well, I'd better go now. I hope you can come here soon.

I love you.

Your son, Abbas

I really wanted to write the truth, but I had promised myself that I would keep the attack a secret.

As I put the letter away to be posted, people began to come downstairs, one by one. Even though the hotel did not offer breakfast, many of the Persians needed tea first thing in the morning. I got to work, also advertising my shoe-cleaning business by mentioning it with every glass of tea that I served.

My head was still scabbing, but it was difficult to see beneath my hair. There was also the scar on my neck from the point of the knife. The most visible was the bruise on my face, though. Some people asked about it, and I told them that I got into a fight with local boys.

After the events of that tragic evening, I had decided that I would confine myself to the hotel even more than before. This, therefore, meant that I could no longer do the package runs for Hector. I decided to go to town now, while it was morning. I really did not want to leave the hotel, but I had to. I had not eaten for two days, and my lira had gone toward the hotel bill. I had not made any money for three days, either.

I did not want any fuss, so I waited for Murat to leave the reception area for a moment, and then I was out the door. My heart was racing, and I was extra aware of everyone around me. In a state of paranoia, I walked briskly down the road with my hands in my pockets, clutching the sixty dollars I had stashed there. I had fifty that I wanted to change, and a marked ten-dollar note that I had to exchange with Hector.

I reached the marketplace and headed straight for Hector's shop. He looked up from examining a piece of jewelry and saw me. He was smiling, but as soon as he saw my face, he turned serious.

"What happened to you, my friend?"

"Nothing," I said, "it was nothing."

"It obviously was," he said in a firm voice. "Who did this to you?"

I did not say anything.

"Who did this to you, Abbas?" he asked more loudly.

"I don't know."

"Don't you protect anyone," he ordered me. "Whoever it was will regret this. I'll take care of it, Abbas. Just tell me who did this to you."

"I don't know," I said softly. "I swear."

"What happened?"

I told him. Hector looked into my eyes. I had never seen him like this before. I thought he was going to kill *me*, never mind that man.

"What did he look like?" he asked.

"I can't really remember. It was dark and I was scared."

"If you ever see this guy again, you come straight here and tell me, okay?"

"Okay."

There was a brief silence as we both got our breath back.

"So will you have a drink, Abbas?" he asked in a more relaxed tone.

"No, thank you," I said. "I just want to change my money and . . . well, I wanted to swap my last marked ten-dollar bill, because I do not want to carry the packages anymore."

"I see," he said. "Why?"

"I just don't, and it has nothing to do with this," I said, pointing to my face.

"Okay."

"Sorry."

"If that is what you want, then no problem."

It was going a little better than I had imagined.

"Thank you," I said as I handed him the sixty dollars.

"But will you do me a favor?"

"Sure," I said.

"Will you make one more drop today, and that will be the last one?"

I stared at him, wanting to refuse, but unable to bring myself to say it.

"It's okay, Abbas. I understand," he said, then joked, "You'd better come back here and swap money, though."

"I will."

"Good, and if you see that guy again, you come straight here, and I will take care of everything for you." He counted out my money and then handed me a bundle of lira notes and a new ten-dollar note.

"Um, could you please swap the ten, too?" I asked.

"Sure." He handed me all the money and I left.

I made my way back to the hotel, in deep thought about why Hector was so concerned for me. I decided to keep walking to the corner shop. It felt very eerie going down the same path again. I closed my eyes and walked briskly until I had gone past the spot of the attack. I reached the shop and began to pick up the usual things, when I noticed the shopkeeper looking at my face suspiciously. He must have thought that I had been up to no good.

I took my things up to my room and had a small meal. When I went back downstairs, Murat was dozing in the television lounge. I made him a glass of tea and left it in front of him in case he woke up.

I spent the rest of my day between the shoe-cleaning box and the bar. It appeared that the guests had missed me. That cheered me up a little. It was nice to be appreciated, even by strangers. At around eight there was a dip in business, and I took a break in front of the television. *Knight Rider* had just started when Murat hurried into the lounge to say there was a call for me.

I rushed to the lobby and into my phone booth. I shut the door behind me and took a deep breath. Two deep breaths. "Hello?"

"Abbas, my darling?" my mother's voice echoed.

"Maman," I screamed, "how are you?"

"I'm good, Sweetness," she said, "and how are you?"

"I'm okay. No, I'm good," I forced out.

"What are you doing?" she asked gently.

"Watching television," I said more cheerfully. *"Knight Rider* is on. It is a great show. Where is Baba?"

"Not in at the moment," she said softly. "Are you really fine?"

"Yes, why?"

"I don't know," she said. "It's just something."

I understood that she felt something was wrong, but luckily, she did not know exactly what.

"No, I'm fine, Maman, I promise." It was very difficult for me to lie to my mother. "Have you got any more letters?" I asked, trying to change the subject.

"Yes, my darling," she said. "I love them. I read them all the time."

I smiled to myself, thinking of how many times I had read her letter to me. "Maman, you had better go," I told her. "Your bill is going to be huge."

My guess was that my father knew nothing of that call, and it had not been planned. With a smile, I returned to *Knight Rider* and actually managed to forget everything for the remainder of the show. For the rest of the evening, I served drinks and mingled with the guests. That night I went to bed feeling tired, hoping for a good night's sleep.

During the next five and a half weeks, I left the hotel only three times a week and only in the mornings, for food. I went to the marketplace twice, and I exchanged more money at a time now, so that I would not have to come back so frequently. Hector was still giving me good rates, and he never mentioned the packages again.

I made myself a prisoner in the hotel, keeping myself busy with my jobs. The backgammon games were not so popular anymore, but they did take place once in a while. The phone calls from my parents were getting less frequent and shorter. It was obvious that my parents were not doing very well with money.

The day of my next consulate meeting inched closer but a lot slower than I had anticipated. I had thought that if I kept myself busy, time would move faster, but no matter what I did, every second felt like an hour. I was continually looking at the date and wishing that the day would arrive.

FIFTEEN

When at last I woke up on the morning of my consulate appointment, I was hoping for some kind of final answer, an end to my wait. I had been in Istanbul for more than two months now.

I stepped off the bus with my heart racing. This afternoon could change everything. This time, I looked over at my consulate friend before going for a ticket, and sure enough, he waved to me. I walked straight to the side door and waited for him. He shook my hand this time and seemed even friendlier than before. It was strange, because the first time I had met this man, he'd seemed so serious.

Once again, I was taken to the door that led into the consul's office. I sat outside, expecting to be there for a good hour, but suddenly the door opened. The consul and the translator were both there. The consul was wearing a navy suit this time, as handsome as his beige one.

"Hello," I said in English.

"Please sit down," he said.

The hot chocolate and the biscuits were waiting for me. The consul pointed to them, indicating that I should help myself.

"Thank you," I said in English again. He smiled, as my minuscule repertoire of English words was on display again.

"The situation is complicated," the translator began. "Your cousin has signed papers to say that he will be your guardian, and that is the most important thing. He has also confirmed that you are going there to avoid being sent to war and for your education. So far, your story has been completely genuine as to your cousin's occupation and other details that we have asked for. But that alone is usually not enough to issue a visa, because everyone would try that approach."

"What does that mean?" I asked apprehensively.

"Well, the consul has suggested that your case be considered much faster than usual because of your situation," he explained. "He has done all the paperwork, and he will write a final report after today's meeting. Then a decision should be made, but once again, he is adamant that you understand there are no guarantees."

"I understand."

"Good."

The translator began to speak to the consul. I looked around again at the rich curios and decorations in his grand office. I did not know whether I should be happy or worried. The one thing that I could tell was that, hopefully, I would get an answer one way or another very soon. The consul smiled at me as the translator continued, "The consul wants to know how you are."

I looked at the consul and said, "Okay."

The consul looked straight back into my eyes and nodded. He stayed quiet for a while and then said something to the translator.

"When did you last speak to your parents?" he asked.

"Four or five days ago," I said. "They have no money now, because we had to sell everything so I could come here."

The translator relayed my words, only to receive another knowing nod from the consul. Then he asked something as he looked at me.

"The consul wants to know if there is anything you want to tell him that may help you."

"I don't know if it will help me," I said, "but please request for him to tell me something soon. I don't know how much longer I can pretend to my parents that I am fine. The last time I was here, I was hungry on my way back and when I went to buy food, I was attacked. A man held me at knife-point, slammed my head against a wall, and punched my face. You can't see the bruises now as they have healed. Please just tell me if I can go to England or not, because I can't sleep. I feel too frightened to go out of the hotel, and I miss my parents. If I go back to Iran, I may get sent to the war. I know that my father would hate me for saying this, but at least I would see my parents before they send me off. So, please, just ask the consul to tell me soon, one way or the other."

The consul suddenly stood up, which immediately made me do the same. He gestured for me to sit down and walked to where I was sitting. He tilted my head, and looking at my neck, placed his index finger exactly where I had been cut. As he did so, he talked to the translator.

"He says that you were very lucky. He says to come back in two weeks, and he will see what he can do for you. He also says you should continue to stay in your hotel."

"Thank you."

With that, the consul showed me to the door, shook my hand, and patted me on the shoulder as if to say, "Hang in there."

I returned to the hotel, disappointed. If they did not give me the visa, what would my father think? This worried me more than not getting the visa. I decided not to tell my parents that the consulate might give me their decision next time. I decided to just tell them that I would have to return there in two weeks.

So for a fortnight, I stayed within the safety of the hotel. I talked to my parents twice very briefly, telling them only that I had to go back for another interview. Those two weeks passed by a lot more swiftly than the previous five had, because this time I was nervous about going back.

When I got off the bus outside the consulate again two weeks later, I felt a cold breeze rush through my hair. Again, my consulate friend saw me when I got inside, and this time he waved me over to his booth. He smiled and said, "Passport."

He took it, and then he handed me a piece of paper and said something I did not understand. He showed me his watch and indicated two hours. I walked outside. I was scared to leave the premises in case they wanted to see my passport when I came back in, but at the gates I showed the guards the paper and two fingers to indicate two hours, and they smiled and nodded.

I walked down the road and found a small park, which was quite empty. It was probably one of the prettiest parks I had ever seen. It was a tiny patch of green, with little benches around a small square. There was an old couple feeding pigeons, and I sat on a bench watching them. Every few minutes, I would look at my watch.

Time seemed to be standing still. After an hour and a half, I could not wait any longer. I decided to return to the consulate.

After my consulate friend finished with his last client, he walked into the back office and re-emerged with the consul. They smiled at me and called me over. My heart was pounding as fast as it had the night I'd been attacked. I walked slowly to the counter. The consul opened my passport without saying anything and showed me a shiny visa in it. He then walked around and opened the side door so that he could give it to me personally. He took my hand in his and said, "Good luck."

"Thank you," I said. "Thank you, too," I repeated to my consulate friend. All of a sudden I had so many conflicting emotions. I wanted to cry for joy; I wanted to laugh out loud; but most of all I wondered: What would my parents think and say? The delight that ran through me was mostly because I knew I was going to please them. I was not scared of disappointing my father anymore. This was the happiest day of my life.

I took my passport and walked out of the building. On the bus, I opened my passport again. It looked so beautiful. The shiny sealed sticker stuck in my passport glowed up at me. It had all been worth it. I could not wait until that night. I was going to call my parents as soon as I got back to the hotel. I ran all the way from the bus stop. Out of breath, I ran into the lobby to find Murat.

"Murat, Murat!" I called out.

"What happened?" he asked.

"I got it! I got it!" I screamed.

"What?"

"My visa," I said as I showed it to him. He jumped off his chair and came to hug me.

"Well done, Little Man. Well done."

"Thank you," I said. "May I call my parents?"

"Sure," he said, "and if you keep it short, it's on me."

"Wow," I said, "thank you."

I wrote down the number for him and ran into the phone booth. I waited, and thirty seconds later my phone rang. I picked it up. After about five rings, my mother was on the line.

"Hello?"

"Maman?"

"Abbas, my darling?" she said, all surprised. "What happened?"

"Nothing, Maman, nothing," I said, trying to calm her down. "I have some news."

"What?"

"I got it! I got the visa!"

The loudest scream came down the phone line. "Oh, my God. That is wonderful!"

"Is Baba there?"

"Karim!" she shouted. "So they've given it to you already?"

"Yes, it is in my passport. I'm looking at it."

"I can't believe it, Abbas," she said. "I never thought this would be possible. You've made me so proud. What you have done is truly amazing. Here is your father."

"Hello?" he said. "What happened?"

"I got the visa today, Baba."

"You're joking."

"No, honestly, I am looking at it right now."

"Abbas, that is brilliant! Well done, my son. You don't know how proud I am."

"You are?"

"Am I? Do you think anyone else could have done this?" he asked seriously.

"I don't know," I said.

"Well, they couldn't have. You should be proud of yourself, Abbas."

Those were the words for which I had waited two and a half months.

"Thank you, Baba."

"Now we have to get you a ticket to London," he said. "How much money do you have left?"

"More than six hundred dollars."

"This gets better and better," he said, laughing. "I will get Mehdi to buy your ticket, and you can pick it up from British Airways in Istanbul. Then, when you get to London, you can pay him with your dollars. I will call you tonight to tell you where to go to pick up your ticket."

"Okay, Baba," I said, smiling to myself. "You go now, because my bill will get huge."

I had the biggest grin on my face. I walked out of the booth to see Murat smiling.

"They were happy, huh?"

"Oh, yes," I said, "just a little bit."

"When are you leaving?"

"I don't know. They are sending a ticket, which I'll have to pick up from British Airways. Do you know where that is?"

"I do. I'll go with you if you want."

"That would be great."

"And one more thing . . . Can I take you to the airport?"

"You'd do that?" I asked. "Thank you."

"My pleasure," he said. "We'll go in my car."

"You have a car?"

"Yes."

"I have known you for more than two months, and I did not know that."

"That's because I am always here." We both laughed.

Sure enough, my father did ring that night. My flight was in five days. I could not believe it. I was actually going to England.

The next five days were spent washing clothes and packing. I got my money from Murat and exchanged the remaining lira back into dollars. In the evenings, I still worked, serving drinks and cleaning shoes. Those five days seemed to last longer than all the weeks I had already been there. I was excited about seeing the country that my father had convinced me was the greatest in the world.

The day of my departure finally came. True to his word, Murat helped me with my bags and took me to the airport in his car. On the way, we were silent. Neither of us knew what to say. Honestly, I knew I was going to miss him. He might have tried to trick me a few times, but he had also saved my life and been a true friend. He was a good guy.

At the airport, I checked in and a lady was sent to look after me.

"Well, Little Man," Murat said, "I guess this is it."

"Yes."

"Who am I going to find to serve tea like you, huh?" He was getting quite emotional, which surprised me.

"You'll find someone."

"Not like you," he said, "and who else is there to keep me on the straight and narrow—and come up with all those crazy business ideas?"

"Only one!"

"A good one."

"Thanks," I said, embarrassed.

"I'll miss you, Little Man. People like you don't come around too often."

"Thank you, Murat. I will miss you, too."

"You take care of yourself."

"You too, Murat. You take care, too."

I could see in his eyes that he really *was* going to miss me. I wondered if he would cry, but that was not Murat's style, and I knew that what we had just said was going to be our farewell. The fact that I was sad made him look at me that extra second longer than he would have otherwise, though. And that extra second's look told me a lot: he cared. With that, he turned and disappeared into the crowd.

The airport was where I had met my first friend in Istanbul. Without Ahmed the taxi driver's help, I might not have lasted one night in that city. Here I was again, losing touch with another friend. This was likely the last time I would ever see Murat. But I would never forget him.

And so came an end to my adventures in Istanbul. The British Airways lady took me straight to the plane, where I sat unable to stop smiling as I looked forward to my future.

Epilogue

initially believed I had fulfilled all of my goals by obtaining a UK visa and reaching English shores. However, I soon realized that hardships can come in all shapes and sizes in all countries, even in developed, first-world countries like England. Unfortunately, my cousin was not a kind man. From the moment he met me at the airport, he made it clear that he wanted nothing to do with me. A few days later, he shipped me off to an English boarding school, which would bring its own challenges of loneliness and abuse. Perhaps England was not the Promised Land after all; but somehow, those three difficult months in Istanbul where I had lived by my wits, often terrified and overwhelmed by loneliness, yet learning to survive in a foreign land, had prepared me for the hard challenges to come.

And so, like Rocky training for the fight of his life in the movie I loved so much, I, too, had trained. And now I was ready.

A Note to Readers

Dear Reader,

Thank you for reading my story. Honestly, I still cannot believe this is a reality—that *my* story, in my own words, is in print! I had three main reasons for writing it: to honor my mother's memory, so that long after I am gone, people will know of her strong character and her many sacrifices; to document a small story that was part of a much larger one, both historically and sociologically; and to commemorate all those Iranians who lost and endured so much during those troubled years in Iran in the early 1980s. There were many stories like mine, and my tale was by no means the most difficult or the most tragic. I am honored each time someone reads this book, because it means they will learn of the hardships so many were forced to face, particularly those who dared to oppose the new regime.

Abbas Kazerooni, California 2012

Acknowledgements

I would like to thank all my friends and family who have helped me along the way and given me their advice throughout this process. It has been a long, hard road. Specifically, I would like to thank Fereydoun, Nadine, and Firooz for adopting me into their family and making all of my opportunities a possibility.

I would like to thank my Australian publishers, Allen & Unwin, and their wonderful editorial team. And now, with this new edition, I thank those at Amazon Children's Publishing for giving me the opportunity to bring my story to the US. I am grateful to Melanie Kroupa for doing such an excellent job of re-editing the book for the American market. Thank you ALL for caring and being true to the voice and integrity of the story.

Most importantly, I would like to thank my biological parents for having the courage to take the chances that they took for my benefit and to their detriment. I am who I am because of what they sacrificed for me.

ABOUT THE AUTHOR

ABBAS KAZEROONI is a lawyer in California. He is also a professional actor, writer, and producer. Shows he has acted in include *Sleuth* on the London stage (lead role); the BBC's *The Land of the Green Ginger* (lead role); HBO's *The Hamburg Cell*; and the independent feature film *Universal Senses*. *On Two Feet and Wings* is his first book.

ON
TWO FEET
AND
WINGS